Cardinal Cahal B. Daly

Bread
of Life

REFLECTIONS ON THE EUCHARIST

Edited by Gemma Loughran

Published 2011 by
Veritas Publications
7–8 Lower Abbey Street
Dublin 1
Ireland
publications@veritas.ie
www.veritas.ie

ISBN 978-1-84730-330-1

10 9 8 7 6 5 4 3 2 1

Cover designed by Dara O'Connor, Veritas
Printed in Ireland by Gemini International, Dublin

Veritas books are printed on paper made from the wood pulp of managed forests. For every tree felled, at least one tree is planted, thereby renewing natural resources.

Contents

Cardinal Cahal B. Daly
Bread of Life: Reflections on the Eucharist

CAHAL DALY, who was born on the Feast of St Thérèse of Lisieux
in 1917 and died on 31 December 2009, was ordained priest in
1941. He served as bishop of Ardagh and Clonmacnoise from
1967 until 1982, when he became bishop of his native diocese
of Down and Connor. In 1990, he was appointed Archbishop of
Armagh and was made Cardinal in 1991. Among his episcopal
objectives were to be a person of prayer and a sanctifier of
his people, to renew the Church in Ireland in the light of the
Second Vatican Council, to have a preferential love for the poor,
to work towards ecumenical reconciliation, to combat political
violence and to search for peace in Northern Ireland. His
writings, many of which have been published by Veritas, ranged
from the pastoral to the spiritual, theological and philosophical.

GEMMA LOUGHRAN met Dr Daly when she was a student of, and
he was a Reader in, Scholastic Philosophy at Queen's University,
Belfast. Their shared interest in philosophy and theology led to the
development of a friendship between them. She is literary executrix
of his estate.

FOREWORD

Although he was aged ninety when he died at the end of 2009, Cardinal Daly continued to 'run the race' in many ways, not least by preparing for publication his theological, spiritual and prayerful insights. He was particularly keen to ensure that, in advance of the Eucharistic Congress in Ireland in 2012, the reflections on the Eucharist which are contained in this book should be available in print.

It was the hope of Cardinal Daly that individuals and groups would find in these reflections rich sources of understanding, prayer, contemplation and practical advice.

The reflections complement the Cardinal's earlier work entitled *The Breaking of Bread: Biblical Reflections*, published by Veritas in June 2008.

We wish to record gratitude to Gemma Loughran who edited and to Nancy McGarry who typed *Reflections on the Eucharist*.

Chapter 1

The Mass, our Pasch

The Mass and the Eucharist are the purpose and the very meaning of the whole of Catholic life. We are created in order to offer Mass; we are baptised in order to offer Mass; we are instructed, catechised, educated in Catholic schools, in order to offer Mass. The laity are never more the laity than when they gather in church around the priest on the altar to offer the sacrifice of the new law, or the new covenant, the sacrifice of the People of God.

The word 'laity' come from the Greek work *laos*, meaning 'the people'. This was the name of the People of God in the Old Testament and, as such, the word inherits all the privileges and purposes of the old chosen people. The old chosen people, the Jews, were delivered by God's mighty hand out of slavery and suffering in Egypt. They were conducted by God's victorious power across the Red Sea, in which their enemies were destroyed, and guided by his loving and protecting presence through the dangers and trials of the desert towards the Promised Land, where he himself would be their God and they would be his people.

The culminating act of God's protection of his people in Egypt was the Pasch, or Passover. In order to force their enemies to let them go free, God had to punish them with various plagues and, in the end, when they still continued stubborn and defiant, he resorted to the terrible visitation of the death of the first-born of every house. But his own people, though living scattered amidst the Egyptians, were to be spared by a special act of divine mercy. If they offered a lamb to God in sacrifice and marked the lintels and doorposts of their houses with its blood, then the wrath of God would pass over and spare them, because God, by the mark of the blood of the paschal lamb, would recognise and save his own.

All this exercise of divine power on behalf of his people had one purpose – that they might offer sacrifice to God. God said to Moses: 'When thou shalt have brought my people out of Egypt, thou shalt offer sacrifice to God upon this mountain'; and God instructed Moses to say to Pharaoh: 'The Lord God of the Hebrews hath called us; we will go three days' journey into the wilderness to sacrifice unto the Lord our God' (Ex 3:18). Every year, the Jews celebrated the memory of that great event by the offering and sacrifice of the paschal lamb and by partaking of its flesh.

When they had crossed the Red Sea and had left their pagan enemies defeated behind, they wandered for forty years through the desert. But first, on Mount Sinai, amidst awe-inspiring thunder and unearthly flame and fire, God showed his presence and enacted the covenant by which he bound himself to them, and them to him, irrevocably: giving them at the same time, in the Commandments, the pattern of life and conduct which alone is becoming to a chosen, consecrated, priestly people.

During their wanderings in the desert, the Jews enjoyed at all times the presence and protection of God:

> The Lord went before them to show the way by day in a pillar of cloud and by night in a pillar of fire, that he might be the guide of their journey at both times. (Ex 13:21)

When they were parched with thirst, God sent water gushing out of a rock at the stroke of Moses' wand (Ex 17:6).

Among other miracles of power and love that God worked for them, two were outstanding. When they were fainting for want of food, he sent them manna from heaven to eat and 'with this meat they were fed until they reached the borders' of the Promised Land, but they were allowed to gather manna only for one day: if they tried to store it up for tomorrow, it rotted (Ex 16:35).

St Paul says: 'All these things happened to them in symbol; and they are written for our instruction, upon whom the ends of the world are come' (1 Cor 10:11). For us, all these figures and types of the Old Testament have become reality and truth. The Jews still celebrate the Passover: there is among them a lovely legend that during Passover meal, some Jewish family will hear a knock and will open the door and find that it is the long-awaited Messiah come at last to join them at their paschal supper. But the truth that we are privileged to know is infinitely more beautiful than the legend, for Christ – the promised one – has come and is with us at our paschal meal today and every day.

Let us read from St John's account of the Last Supper:

> Before the festival day of the Pasch, Jesus, knowing that his hour was come that he should pass out of this world to the Father, having loved his own who were in the world, he loved them unto the end. (Jn 13:1)

Note that it was at the Passover meal that he instituted the Blessed Eucharist, the new Pasch, as a memorial and sign of his own passing over out of this world to his Father. The Eucharist, sacrifice and sacrament, is the means whereby we are enabled to pass through this world with Christ, and in him to return to the Father. The Mass is precisely *the life* of a Christian, of a christened one, one who lives in Christ and walks with Christ and dies in Christ so as to be received back with him into the embrace of the eternal Father.

THE MASS, OUR PASCH

The Mass is our Pasch. In it we offer to God the paschal lamb that was slain on the cross for our sins and we receive his flesh, which was given back to the Father in death for our salvation. In the

Mass we are marked, cleansed, purified by the blood of the lamb, consecrated and set apart by it as God's chosen people. The Mass gathers us in, out of the sinfulness of the surrounding world, and then sends us out again into that world to tell it of Christ's truth and bring it to Christ's love. The Mass sets us apart as God's people. We read that Moses,

> taking the book of the covenant, read it in the hearing of the people, and they said: 'All things that the Lord has spoken we will do, we will be obedient.' And Moses took the blood and sprinkled it upon the people and he said: 'This is the blood of the covenant which the Lord has made with you. (Ex 24:7-8)

Whenever we attend Mass, at the Consecration we hear the priest say: 'This is the Blood of the new and eternal covenant which shall be shed for you and for many unto the remission of sins.' The Blood of the Eucharistic Lamb marks us as God's own; like the brand of a sheep which enables it to be found or returned when strayed, it enables the Good Shepherd to recognise and claim us in life and in death as belonging to him. When we pray for the dying, we say: 'May Christ, the Good Shepherd, claim you as one of his flock.'

The divine judgement will spare those marked with the Eucharistic Blood. St Paul says there is no judgement for those who are in Christ Jesus:

> Who can be our adversary, if God is on our side? He did not even spare his own Son, but gave him up for us all; and must not that gift be accompanied by the gift of all else? Who will come forward to accuse God's elect, when God acquits us? Who will pass sentence against us, when Jesus Christ, who died, nay who has risen again, and sits at the right hand of God, is pleading for us? Who will separate us from the love of Christ? (Rom 8:31-35)

Jesus himself said that, at the last judgement, when people are withering away due to fear and dread, his followers are to look up with eagerness and joy, for it will be their redemption that is at hand (Lk 21:25-28). For Jesus' followers, the judgement will simply be him coming to look for his own to claim them for himself and bring them home with him to his Father. Indeed the Mass *is* our judgement. 'Now is the judgement of the world,' Our Lord said, 'now shall the prince of this world be cast out. And I, if I be lifted up from the earth, will draw all things to myself.' St John comments: 'Now this he said, signifying what death he should die' (Jn 12:31-33). At the Consecration and the Elevation of the Mass, this lifting up of Jesus on the cross and to the Father are renewed, and the judgement of the world – which is the separating of us out from the sinful world, and the sparing of us from the world's condemnation – is re-enacted. In order to escape condemnation, we only need to be truly the people of the Mass. Our Lord said: 'I came not to judge the world, but to save the world' (Jn 12:47). And again: 'He who heareth my word and believeth him who sent me, hath life everlasting; and cometh not into judgement, but is passed from death to life' (Jn 5:24).

Note the recurrence of the words 'passed (over) from death to life'. The reason why the Mass *is* our life and our salvation is because we grasp and hold in it the Body and Blood of Christ who has passed from death to life, out of this world to the Father. And he has done so for us in order that in him, with him and through him we too may come to the Father. On the cross he loved us to the end and the consummation; he loved the Father for our sake, adored him in our name, atoned to him for our sins. On the cross, 'with a strong cry and with tears he offered up prayers and supplications' for our sake to the Father who could save him, and us with him, from death. And he 'was heard for his reverence': because of his filial love, his cry of love was heard and 'being consummated, he became, to all that obey him, the cause of eternal salvation' (Heb 5:7-9).

The proof that he was heard was the resurrection: the Father took him up in glory to his own right hand, and there he is the source, pledge and guarantee of our salvation. In Mass we have and hold the Body, which is already in glory at the Father's side. We touch and taste the Blood, which speaks to the Father of an infinite love that has risen from earth and pierced the heavens. The Mass brings us to where he is already: in the Father's arms. The Mass is the Christian journey completed, the Christian life consummated. In the Mass, as on Calvary, all is consummated.

In St John's Gospel it is recorded that Jesus said on the cross, 'It is consummated' and, 'bowing his head, he gave up the ghost' (Jn 19:30). Some commentators see a deeper meaning in these words. They follow immediately after Jesus' words to Mary and to John: 'Woman, behold thy son' and 'Son, behold thy mother.' In this context, the words 'bowing his head, he gave up the ghost' could mean: 'turning his head towards Mary and John, he handed on to them the Holy Spirit.' They could mean that Jesus, in death, is sending the Holy Spirit upon the Church, represented here by Mary, its mother, and John, its priest and faithful disciple. John himself realised that the Church was born at that moment from the side of Christ. In awestruck tones, he tells us that he saw the soldier strike Christ's side with a spear and saw blood and water gush out from that side. John is recalling the rock in the desert from which water gushed at the touch of Moses' rod. He is recalling also Our Lord's words, which he had earlier quoted, words spoken in the temple on the feast of tabernacles:

> If any man thirst, let him come to me and drink, he that believeth in me, as the Scripture saith, 'Out of his bosom will flow rivers of living water'. (Jn 7:37-8)

Describing further the piercing with a lance of Our Lord's body on the cross, John quotes the prophet Zechariah: 'They shall look on him whom they pierced' (Jn 19:37). This passage from Zechariah says:

> I will pour out upon the house of David and upon the inhabitants of Jerusalem the spirit of grace and of prayers: and they shall look upon me whom they have pierced ... (Zech 12:10)

It is very similar, of course, to the passage from the prophet Joel that St Peter took for the text of the first Christian sermon on the first Pentecost: 'I will pour out my spirit upon all flesh.' Peter went on to say:

> This Jesus ... you, by the hands of wicked men, have crucified and slain ... This Jesus hath God raised again. Being exalted therefore by the right hand of God and having received of the Father the promise of the Holy Ghost, he hath poured forth this which you see and hear. (Acts 2:23, 32-33)

It is because Jesus has been raised in resurrected glory to the Father's right hand that we can receive the life and pardon and consolation and confidence of the Holy Spirit. After the words I have quoted about the feast of the tabernacles, St John goes on:

> Now this he said of the Spirit which they should receive who believed in him: for as yet the Spirit was not given, because Jesus was not yet glorified. (Jn 7:39)

But now Jesus is glorified. The Spirit is given. And in the Mass we have in our midst the glorified Body of Jesus, and from his pierced heart we receive rivers of living water, the outpoured gifts and graces of his Holy Spirit. Mass renews Pentecost as it renews the passion and the resurrection and the ascension. Having given us Christ in the Mass, with him God has also given us all things

(Rom 8:32). In the Mass, to use St Paul's words, 'all things are yours
... and you are Christ's; and Christ is God's' (1 Cor 3:22-23). In
these days of the passionate call for the working of the Holy Spirit
in the Church, it is well to recall this connection between Mass and
the outpouring of the Holy Spirit.

THE PEOPLE OF THE MASS

Let us be, then, more and more the people of the Mass. At this time of
doubt and insecurity, of change and instability, of neo-paganism and
materialism, of irreligion and irreligious propaganda, let us gather in
more tightly around Christ in the Mass. The Mass is the only thing
we have that is worthy of being given to God, the only offering we
have that God cannot refuse. Even our sinful hands cannot soil it;
even our shabby lives cannot spoil it: the Mass is the one thing on
earth we cannot ruin. For the Mass is the crucified but glorified
Body of Christ, the suffering, but also the victory, of the Son of God.

The Mass is the offering of the whole People of God. The
wonderful privilege whereby all can join vocally in the prayers of
the Mass in the vernacular, underlines the fact that we all offer Mass
together. I want to refer to another aspect of 'we all': the 'we' who
offer Mass includes the saints in heaven, our Blessed Lady in chief
and the canonised saints, but also all those of all the generations
past who have fought the good fight in their time and have now
passed out of the world and are in Christ with the Father. We speak
much nowadays of the 'Church of the future'. But the Church is
also, and must ever remain, the Church of fidelity to the past. The
Communion of Saints makes us one across the centuries with all
the generations who have kept faith with Christ. They built our
churches for us, they kept the faith for us, they handed on the faith
to us. At Mass they are with us praying that we may 'continue in
the faith, grounded and settled and immovable from the hope of the
Gospel' (Col 1:23).

We are the people of the Mass. The completion of Mass is our Holy Communion, when the Body we have offered to the Father is given back to us by him in order that by it he may share with us his heavenly life. This is the true manna, the true bread from heaven which Jesus promised his Father would give us and which gives life to the world (Jn 6:32-33). As with the manna, what the Father gives is enough for all the needs of any day. Our Lord taught us to pray for this day's bread, not to worry anxiously about tomorrow's. Tomorrow is another day, another Mass, another Holy Communion. Sufficient for today is this day's Mass, this day's Eucharistic bread.

THE BODY OF THE LORD

We are privileged now, as we receive Holy Communion, to answer 'Amen' to the priest's 'Body of Christ' when we receive Holy Communion. This Amen can be a renewal of our whole Christian faith. By it, we can mean, 'Yes, I believe this *is* the Body of Christ, pierced for me on the cross, living now with the Father. Yes, I accept this Body and I stake on it all my hopes in life and in death. Yes, Lord, I will let you into my whole being, into the whole of my life; I will close no door to you, keep nothing back from you, refuse nothing to you. Yes Lord, I accept your Body; and here is mine in return, for you to own and use and make free of as it pleases you. Make it like your own, make it yours, even if that has to hurt. Live in me so that I can say "I live, now not I, but Christ liveth in me" (Gal 2:20).' As St Thérèse of Lisieux said: 'Anything you ask, Lord, only have pity for me.' Come, Lord Jesus. Amen. May it be so.

The Blessed Eucharist is our individual food. It is also the food and strength of the whole Church. In the twelfth chapter of Revelations, the 'woman clothed with the sun' is both Mary and the Church. We read that the dragon, the devil, persecuted the woman and that there were given to the woman two wings of a great eagle that she might fly into the desert unto her place, where she is nourished for a time and times and half a time. (Rev 12:14)

The eagle is God, whom we read of in the Canticle of Moses, finding his people 'in a desert land in a place of horror and of vast wilderness' and keeping them as the apple of his eye and hovering over them like the eagle teaching his young to fly, spreading his wings and carrying them on his shoulders (Deut 32:10-11). So does God feed his Church with the Blessed Eucharist in the wilderness and danger of this world. The woman is also Mary. She too was nourished on earth with the Flesh of him whom she bore in her womb, and she will help us to see the blessed fruit of her womb in the Blessed Sacrament Jesus Christ.

Jesus Christ in the Blessed Sacrament is above all and always the sacrificial victim offered, received back and eaten in this sharing of the life of God, this passing over of ourselves into the embrace of God, which is the Christian life. But he is also reserved in our tabernacles as our ever really present Lord for our adoration. The idea is sometimes encountered that devotion to the real presence in the tabernacle is less stressed now than it was formerly, or that it is somehow less than strictly liturgical. This idea is very foolish. Adoration of the Most Blessed Sacrament is the proof in practice that we hold the faith of the early Fathers: St Ignatius, St Irenaeus, St Cyril of Jerusalem, St Cyril of Alexandria, St Gregory of Nyssa, St Augustine. Adoration of the Most Blessed Sacrament is the test by life and deeds of our commitment to the reality behind the Council of Trent's words which sum up that faith of the early Fathers:

After the consecration of the bread and the wine, our Lord Jesus Christ, true God and true man, is truly, really and substantially present beneath the appearance of these sensible elements.

ADORATION OF THE BLESSED SACRAMENT

Adoration of the Most Blessed Sacrament is part of our participation on earth in the heavenly liturgy, in which the great multitude of the redeemed, standing before the throne in the presence of the lamb, cries with a loud voice:

> To our God, who sits on the throne, and to the lamb, all saving power belongs … Amen, blessing and glory and wisdom and thanksgiving and honour and power and strength belong to our God through endless ages. Amen. (Rev 7:12)

'Power and Godhead, wisdom and strength, honour and glory and blessing are his by right, the lamb that was slain' (Rev 5:12). The vision of the Seer in these passages is shifting continually from the earthly processions of white-robed new-baptised, passing with lighted candles in their hands from the baptistery to the altar to offer for the first time the sacrifice of the Eucharistic Lamb, upwards to the heavenly triumph of white-robed martyrs, with palm-branches in their hands, chanting for ever the praises of the Lamb that was slain and has redeemed us in his Blood 'out of every tribe and tongue and people and nation, and made us to our God a kingdom and priests' (Rev 5:9-10).

Adoration of the Most Blessed Sacrament begins in the Mass itself. Everything that is said and done at Mass, from the Consecration to the Communion, is marked by veneration of the real presence of the Body and Blood of Christ in the Sacred Species. Benediction, forty hours' prayer, holy hours, visits to the Blessed Sacrament, Eucharistic processions, Eucharistic congresses, are only extensions of this most solemn and sacred moment of the Mass. Devotion to the Blessed Sacrament, someone has said, is the Mass held in meditation. Indeed, unless the Mass and Holy Communion are held in meditation, first by personal thanksgiving after Mass and then by prayerful devotion before the tabernacle, the liturgy itself could become only routine word and mechanical gesture. The bread of the Eucharist is also the bread of faith. Our Lord said: 'He that eateth my Flesh and drinketh my Blood hath everlasting life' (Jn 6:54). He also said: 'He that heareth my word and believeth him that sent me hath life everlasting' (Jn 5:24). So faith must be nourished – especially faith in Christ's real presence in the Eucharist – otherwise even the Mass and the Blessed Eucharist themselves will avail us nothing. They can be the bread of life to us only if they are first the bread of faith.

The way to nourish faith is by prayer, earnest personal prayer and especially contemplative prayer, but, above all, prayer before the tabernacle. Throughout the journeying of life the Blessed Sacrament is for us what the pillar of cloud by day and the pillar of fire by night were to the Israelites: the guide of our journey at all times, the assurance that we need neither fear the terror of all night nor the arrow that flies by day (Ps 90:5-6), but shall securely pass with Christ through this world to the Father. Once indeed, as St Paul reminds us, we were estranged from the Father, 'our minds alienated from him by a life of sin':

> But now he has used Christ's natural body to win us back through his death, and so to bring us into his presence, holy, and spotless and unreproved. But that means that we must be true to our faith, grounded in it, firmly established in it; nothing must shift us away from the hope we found in the Gospel we once listened to. (Col 1:21-23)

So, as St Paul says, let us not be sad or frightened. We have the Mass and the Blessed Sacrament and that is all we need:

> Wherefore lift up the hand which hangs down and the feeble knees ... For you are come to Mount Sion and the city of the living God, the heavenly Jerusalem; and to the company of

many thousands of angels and to the Church of the first-born who are written in the heavens, and to God the judge of all … and to Jesus, the mediator of the New Testament and to the sprinkling of all blood which speaketh better than that of Abel … Therefore receiving an immovable kingdom, we have grace; whereby let us serve, pleasing God, with fear and reverence. For our God is a consuming fire. (Heb 12)

Chapter 2

Mass and the World of Work

RELIGION AND LIFE

There are basic things about Christianity that are sometimes forgotten. Firstly, we believe it *because it is true*. It is not enough to believe Christianity because it gives consolation in sorrow, strength in adversity, peace of soul, because it is part of our culture, because it gives sound training to our children. We believe Christianity because it is true; nothing can ever shake its truth. Secondly, the truth of Christianity is given to us, not to provide a satisfying explanation of the world and of our own existence, nor to give us a sound and sane morality. Christianity is for living, not just for knowing. Christianity is for doing, not just for listening. Jesus said we must listen to his words and act on them (Mt 7:24-27). Christianity is not about explaining the world, but about changing it. It is not about explaining human existence, but about making us new creatures.

The Bishops of Ireland wrote a Pastoral Letter on Justice in 1977. In it they said:

> One of the urgent needs in the Church today is to remove the partitions separating religion from life and tending to keep religion confined to Sundays and to churches. We must bring the faith into everyday life. We must take religion out into the streets, the factories, the offices, and the farms.

The Bishops appealed to people not to be 'Sunday Christians' only, 'isolating their worship from their weekly lives'. In September 1979, when Ireland was preparing for the Pope's visit, the Irish Bishops said in a Pastoral Letter:

The Holy Father's visit will help us to realise that faith is proved by life; that one cannot be a Christian only on Sundays and only on our knees. We must be Monday to Saturday Christians too. We must be Christians at work, in business, in buying and selling and tax-paying, at employer and trade union meetings, in public and in private life ... The Pope's visit will call us to a new sense of justice, a new respect for the dignity and the rights of every man and woman and particularly of the poor. His coming can help to give our whole country a new sense of purpose, a new pride in honest work, a new desire to pull together as a people to end injustice and degrading poverty in our country.

As we read these words today, can we avoid a feeling of embarrassment and shame that so little did change after the Holy Father's visit? Where now is that 'new sense of purpose', that 'new desire to pull together'? How much have we done to end injustice and degrading poverty in our country? Was it all words, words, words, and very little deeds? Was it all promises, promises, promises, and very few performances?

After the Pope's visit, the Irish Bishops issued a further Pastoral Letter on 'Handing on the Faith in the Home' (1980). This was intended as a direct follow-up to the papal visit. In it, the Bishops said:

We must put our lives where the prayer of our mouth is. Young people in their teens are very sensitive to the contradiction between the way adults go to church and pray, and want young people to behave, and the way they live themselves. Nothing is said more often by teenagers than that they are 'turned off' religion by what they see as the 'hypocrisy' in the religion of many adults ... The reactions of teenagers should make us all conscious of the need to close the gaps between our devotions and our lives, between our prayers and our behaviour, between our Sunday Christianity and our Monday to Saturday living.

THE 'MORNING OFFERING'

Down many generations, a tried and proven way of bringing religion into life and turning prayer into deeds has been the 'Morning Offering'. All the work and words and actions, the prayers and the sufferings of the day, were offered to God before the day's work began, so that the works of the day would be prayer and praise of God continued in another form.

If the work itself is carelessly and badly done, there is no way that prayer is going to make it good. If the work done or the thing made does not praise God in itself by being well done or well made, then it still will not be praising God, even when we pray before it or after it, even if we were to sprinkle holy water upon it!

Thank God, many people do pray well in Ireland. But a lot of the work that people are paid good money to do is botched and badly done, or is not done at all; yet the money is collected just the same. There has to be something wrong with the way we understand prayer and the way we understand Christianity. Our prayer should be the expression of our lives. Our lives should be the continuation of our prayer. The 'morning offering' is still an excellent way to begin the day. Conditions of work, and ways of getting to work through the long traffic lanes, do not make morning prayer easy nowadays. But God is near: no further away than his whispered name, 'Our Father'; and Mary is as close as a silent 'Hail Mary' – even in a traffic jam!

IN UNION WITH THE MASS

Our greatest prayer, our supreme act of worship, is the holy sacrifice of the Mass. In many forms of the 'morning offering', we offer the day's work 'in union with all the Masses that shall be offered up this day all over the world'. When we can get to daily Mass, as many people do, whether before work or at lunch break or in the evening, this gives a very special 'value added' aspect to our work and to our day.

Our Mass should not be a thing apart from life. We do not step aside from weekday living in order to step into church for Sunday Mass. We bring our Sunday Mass out into factory or farm or mart, into business or office or workplace. At the Offertory of the Mass, our gifts, especially bread and wine, are brought up and laid on the altar. They are then transformed into the greatest offering ever made to God from this earth – the sacrificial self-offering made by Christ on the altar of the Cross for our salvation. Offering the bread, the priest says:

> Blessed are you, Lord, God of all creation. Through your goodness we have this bread to offer, which earth has given and human hands have made. It will become for us the bread of life.

Offering the wine, the priest says:

> Blessed are you, Lord, God of all creation. Through your goodness we have this wine to offer, fruit of the vine and work of human hands. It will become our spiritual drink.

THE MASS AND WORK

Bread and wine are the result of God's creation, and also the result of the work of men and women. Farmers, agronomers, technicians, scientists, manufacturers, transport workers, traders, bakers, bread-servers, dieticians, cooks and caterers: all are involved in the production and distribution of bread. A similar variety of workers are involved in the production and distribution of wine. Their work, all work, our work, is laid on the altar and is offered to God with the bread and wine at Mass, to be changed into the Body and Blood of Christ, and thus to be used by him for the redemption of the world.

All work should be such as to be fit to be offered to God. It should be worthy to share in the work of the redemption. What 'human hands have made' must be honestly and truthfully made:

else it is not fit to stand on Christ's altar, it is not worthy to be brought into the Mass. The 'work of human hands' must be honest and dependable: else it is not fit to pour into the chalice, it is not worthy to be brought into the Mass.

I have said Mass myself sometimes in a Benedictine monastery in the Marne county in France. The convent chapel has large windows looking out on the broad, flat wheatfields and the rich vineyards of Champagne. At harvest and vintage time, the Sisters work for the local farmers in these fields and vineyards. Their work and their Mass interweave into one single fabric of life. Their hands gather the sheaves of wheat that make the altar bread, which becomes Christ's Body 'given up for them'. Their hands pick the grapes that make the altar wine, which becomes Christ's Blood 'shed for them and for all men so that sins may be forgiven'.

That should be true also of our lives and of our work. We must bring the Mass out into our weekday life and work, so as to make them fit for God, to be placed on our altar and offered with Christ in our Mass. We must bring our life and work into Mass, to offer it to God in union with Christ's offering. But first we must make our life and work fit to be presented to God. As Christians, we must try to live 'joined up' lives, where our public worship, our personal prayer and our working lives form a consistent unity.

At the end of Mass, we are told: 'The Mass is ended: go in peace.' In another sense, the Mass is beginning, the Mass of life, the Mass of work. We are the people of the Mass. That means that we go out from Mass so to live and so to work, that we live and work in peace – peace with God, peace with our own conscience, peace with our fellow men. The necessary condition for that peace is justice. Justice requires honest work for a just wage, an honest article for a just price. If we do not practice justice then our offering of Mass will be dishonest, as much as our work or trade are dishonest. We will be trying to cheat God. In the Bible, there are repeated warnings against offering dishonest sacrifices, against cheating in our worship.

God is not cheated. St Paul says: 'Don't delude yourselves ... into thinking God can be cheated' (Gal 6:7). 'Two-timing' is a despicable way to behave in a relationship; we must not 'two-time' God.

INDUSTRIAL PEACE

One would expect that a country whose people come together in great numbers on Sunday mornings to offer Mass would surely be marked to a special degree by justice and peace in industry. The people who are sent from Mass on Sunday with the words 'Go in peace' should not be the first and the quickest to call for industrial strife on Monday. There must indeed be justice in industry; but there are more peaceful ways than strikes, there are more Christian ways than conflict for securing justice.

Justice also includes those outside the factory floor – the public, the poor, other workers, the unemployed and their children, the job-seeking youth. When we remember the urgent need for real increases in productivity and in competitiveness in Ireland now and recall the link between the Mass and work, it is surely strange that the word 'productivity' today would seem to have little enough to do with actual production, that it is used instead just as a formula for higher-wage claims. Meanwhile, what people in the street experience is often an inferior service for the public and higher prices for the consumer.

Wage levels and wage claims should be related to justice. Instead, they seem to be decided by power and the determination to use power regardless of the consequences for others and for the country. Formerly, employers had all the power, some abused it grossly and workers suffered. Now workers have power too. Some workers have more power than others. Workers nowadays can abuse power just as often and just as much as employers once did. Those with greater power have the greater temptation to abuse it. Too often they forget the effects of their action on their fellow workers who are weaker than themselves, as well as on the poor and the old, the unskilled and the unorganised.

STRIKES

We need, as Christians, to inform our consciences properly about the morality of strikes and the conditions for a just strike. These were set out clearly in the Bishops' Pastoral on Justice. They are often forgotten. In many situations of industrial confrontation, the seriousness of our economic difficulties, the vulnerability of our whole standard of living, do not seem to be grasped. Some industrial disputes seem totally unjustifiable, some pretexts for wage claims seem indefensibly frivolous, given the hardship they inflict upon the public, given the damage they wreak upon the economy, given the threat they cause to other workers' jobs, given the effect they have on the purchasing power of the poor. What can a Christian say, for example, about many of the claims for 'disturbance money'? In how many cases is there any real 'disturbance' or real loss? How often is the term merely a smooth and clever word for a chance of a 'rip-off'? Who pays for the 'rip-off'? Are workers and their leaders confident they can stand before the God of truth and justice and defend the truthfulness and honesty of many of the claims made under such pretexts?

There are strikes that are immoral; which means there are strikes that are sinful. The sin can be grievous. The gains from unjust strikes are ill-gotten gains. How can Christian workers, shop stewards and trade union leaders conduct negotiations on a pay claim, discuss the pros and cons of a strike, or call a strike or place a picket without anyone even raising the question among them whether the strike is morally right or wrong?

Back in 1969, a trade union leader who was a staunch campaigner for workers' rights, but who was first a conscientious Christian, spoke about a strike then dragging on for many months. This was the late Senator James Dunne, then General Secretary of the Maritime Port and General Workers' Union and President of the Irish Congress of Trade Unions. He said to his fellow workers and fellow trade unionists:

Let each one ask himself today if the continuance of this strike is in conscience justified. If their answer is no, well then, let them stand up and say so, however loud the clamour of others. Power carries with it a grave responsibility and its improper or selfish use could well be self-destructive. Any fool may start a strike; it takes men of intelligence and courage to end it.

Why does one so seldom hear or read that kind of language today from a trade union leader? Surely we do not imagine that we leave our Christianity outside on the coat rack when we go into a trade union meeting or an Employer-Labour Conference or a meeting of the 'social partners'.

EMPLOYERS' OBLIGATIONS IN JUSTICE

Employers are bound by the law of justice, no less than workers. Sometimes the language used by or about businessmen and employers would seem to suggest that they are public benefactors, conferring a favour on society because they create jobs and increase the gross national product. But employers also create profits for themselves. These can be very large. They also manufacture wealth for themselves. The wealth is sometimes very great, and the contrast between it and the life of the poor in today's Ireland is vast, and it cannot be justified.

Profits and wealth are not wrong, on condition that they are justly acquired, and on condition that they are justly used. Businessmen and women or employers cannot claim a right to use wealth as they please. Their wealth carries social obligations. Society helped them to acquire it. Society has a right to a share of it. Grants, subsidies and tax breaks provided by taxpayers account for a great part of the wealth of wealthy people. Some wealthy people derived their wealth from clever financial dealing, with no benefit at all to society. The wealthy cannot dispose of this money without keeping in mind the common good of the country, the rights of others and the needs of the poor.

The wealthy have power and opportunity, social standing and influence in high places. With all this comes greater temptation and also greater moral obligation. Clever ways are available to the better-off for successful speculation and sharp business practice. Sophisticated ways are open to well-off groups for unjust tax evasion and concealment of earnings. They must take note of Gospel warnings. The Gospel says firmly: 'What does it profit a man if he gains the whole world and suffers the loss of his soul' (Mt 16:26).

Wealth brings power. It brings political influence. Power carries with it temptation. One of the great sources of temptation in modern society is the temptation to abuse power for selfish gain and to use political influence for business advantage or personal profit. The Gospel is a mirror where all of us can see our warts and our faults. Our Lord has words of truth which expose the humbug in us all. There are words of Our Lord that the rich must specially ponder: 'It will be hard for the rich to enter the Kingdom of Heaven' (Mt 19:23). Wealth can be redeemed. But it needs to be redeemed. It is redeemed by observance of justice and by charity; but justice must have priority even over donations to charitable causes. The first call on employers' profits and property is the just rights of workers and the furtherance of the good of society by better work conditions and increased employment, and by greater respect for the dignity of others. It is good to have factories blessed by religious ceremonies at their opening. It is no less important to have them blessed by good working conditions and just industrial relations after the blessing. It is good to have Mass celebrated on a factory floor: I have often done this myself and I would love to see this happen more often. It is no less important to have the work efficient and honest, the product up to standard, the personnel respected and justly and fairly treated – because the personnel are in the image of God, and God is honoured when their dignity and rights are respected.

PRODUCTION AT THE SERVICE OF JUSTICE

This country has grave economic problems. We need more employment if our splendid young people are to get jobs. We need more production if the young are to get a good educational deal and the old are to get justice.

Government cannot solve the country's problems unless all sections play their part. We must produce and export if we are to survive. If we do not export products, then we will again be exporting people. Unless our work standards and our costs are competitive, hundreds lose jobs and everyone becomes poorer. And the weakest, as always, suffer most of all.

Management as well as workers are responsible for rising costs. Sometimes workers and their wage claims take all the blame, but bad and inefficient management is often at fault too. Poor industrial relations on the side of management causes many strikes and hampers productivity. There can be abuse of company time and company expense accounts; there can be ostentatious executive living. These abuses accord ill with calls to workers for wage restraint.

Neither workers nor management should ever forget that our young and old people depend entirely on their honesty and efficiency. There are many calls for income restraint. There is only one section of society who have to practice income restraint, because they have no other option. They have no bargaining power. They are our pensioners and social welfare recipients. Their only lobby, their only political muscle, is our Christian conscience. Does the voice of conscience, does the voice of justice, have political 'clout' in Ireland? Are there votes in a fair deal for the underprivileged, for those with disabilities, for the old, for mothers working in the home as well as for mothers working outside the home? Are there votes in school classrooms, class sizes, pupil–teacher ratios? These questions challenge us all as voters and challenge politicians.

CHRISTIANS AND A GENERAL ELECTION

When a general election comes round, candidates will canvass our votes. Many interest groups will seek commitments from them on various interests and claims affecting their group. What questions shall we ask the candidates? Whose claims shall we press upon them? It would be scarcely natural if we pressed no personal or sectoral claims. But it would certainly not be Christian if we pressed *only* personal or sectoral claims.

THE THIRD WORLD

Shall we ignore the Third World when election time comes round? We remember it during Lent by supporting the Trócaire Lenten Fast Campaign. That is a Christian thing to do. But we should remember the Third World also at election time, for that too is a Christian thing to do. Shall we think of asking the candidates where they stand and where their parties stand in respect of government aid to the Third World? We rightly fear recession in our own economy, but what we call 'recession' in Ireland, even in today's hard times, would be unimaginable prosperity for millions in the Third World. Yet they are our brothers and sisters. We are their 'keepers'. They are the 'little ones' of Christ. Christ entrusts them to the keeping of our consciences. To borrow the words of Péguy: 'What will he say to us if we come back to him without the little ones?'

THE POOR AND DEPENDENT AT HOME

So far as our own country is concerned, when election time comes round, shall we ask politicians for specific commitments regarding old age and widows' pensions, children's allowances, unemployment benefits (especially for the long-term unemployed), welfare payments and benefits for deserted wives or husbands and single-parent families? Shall we raise with politicians the question of the forgotten men and women who are homeless, who 'sleep out' and 'live rough'? Shall we ask politicians where they stand on the matter of alcohol legislation, and our interference-free enforcement? Shall we make an issue of children's allowances, and ask the question whether society today does enough to support marriage and the family, or if it effectively discriminates against the larger family?

Experts have gravely warned us about the difficulties we shall face as a nation in sustaining our education services, and much more in improving them, given our very large school-going population. Shall we ask politicians for specific promises in respect of educational budgets, school transport, equality of educational opportunity for all areas of the country and for the poorer sectors of the population, and for children with disabilities? Shall we ask candidates their intentions in respect of services for youth, such as recreational facilities, healthy and safe leisure amenities, youth clubs, youth leaders and leadership training courses, and public money to support voluntary effort in all domains affecting our youth?

There has been a saying in political circles: 'There are no votes in education.' Is this true? Are we prepared to make an issue of adequate educational budgeting for the sake of the future of our youth, the future of our country? How much longer must we tolerate sub-standard school buildings? Is the secondary school sector less favourably treated in terms of school grants than other sectors, and, if so, is this fair?

Are there votes in pensions and in welfare benefits? That depends on voters and on their sense of Christian values and priorities. In an age when budgets have to be trimmed and estimates slashed, it depends on Christian voters to use their votes to make sure that cuts are not directed against people with no property and no power – namely the old, the sick, the poor, the young and the people of the Third World. The consciences of Christians must be the lobby, the pressure group, the protest march, on behalf of those who have no voice and no voting strength.

It is earnestly to be hoped that at election time in this Christian country, we will hear much less of the cry 'What will you promise me? What will you do for us?', and much more of the call 'What do you promise the old, the sick and the poor? What will you do for the needy? What will you do for education and our youth? What will you do in respect of world debt and world poverty? What will you do on environmental issues?'

ELECTION ISSUES

Elections tend to be marked by 'issues'. Let us pause and mentally review the issues that have decided elections in the past. How often were they concerned with selfish 'goodies', 'something for nothing' and 'good times ahead for all', with no need to retrain or work harder or save, but only to 'Vote for X'?

How seldom were matters of social justice or a fair deal for the poor, the people in the slums, the homeless and the old, made into election issues? How seldom and by how few politicians were elections made into occasions for challenging the social conscience of our people, and calling them to the sacrifice and the effort needed to build a just society – a society of which a Christian people need not be ashamed?

For far too long we have encouraged the politics of promises, by voting for those politicians or parties who promised the most to us, to our country or village or our interest group. We must make a determined effort next time to support the politics of justice, by voting for those politicians or parties whose platform and whose record are concerned with justice for all sectors of society, and particularly for the under-privileged. That is the true patriotism for today. That is the true republican tradition. As James Connolly put it, the man who is 'bubbling over with love and enthusiasm for Ireland' and yet can pass unmoved through our streets without burning to end 'all the wrong and the suffering, the shame and the degradation ... is a fraud and a liar in his heart', however loudly he professes his love for the country.

POLITICS AND THE CHRISTIAN

Above all, the politics of justice is the only politics worthy of the Christian person. It is the politics of the Sermon on the Mount. It is the politics of the Beatitudes. It is the politics by which, in the end, we shall all of us be judged, voters as well as politicians. For 'as long as we did these things to one of the least of these brothers [of Jesus Christ] we did it to him' and 'in so far as we neglected to do these things to one of the least of these, we neglected to do it to him' (Mt 25:40, 45).

MASS AND POLITICS

All that I have been saying is a direct consequence of the Christian Gospel; it is a straight implication of the meaning of the Mass. At Mass, we have in our midst Christ, who is the Brother of all men and women, but who is especially the Brother of the poor. We celebrate Mass in union with Mary, the lowly virgin whom God 'lifted up' while 'casting the mighty from their thrones'. In honouring Mary, Jesus shows his love and reverence for the poor. In her, 'He fills the starving with good things,' while 'sending the rich empty away.' Can we sincerely offer Mass in union with Mary if we line ourselves up with the powerful, and let the poor be sent empty away?

At Mass, we pray that 'all of us who share in the Body and Blood of Christ be brought together in unity by the Holy Spirit'. We pray that 'we may grow in love' in union with the whole Church. We pray that 'the pilgrim Church on earth' may be 'strengthened in faith and love'. How can our Mass be sincere if we are not trying to build in this country of ours a society of brotherhood, love and compassion?

At Mass, standing in line with all our brothers and sisters, we receive Jesus. Jesus gives his whole attention and love, his whole life, his whole self, to each one in line regardless of income bracket or style or address and irrespective of education or social class. Can we worthily receive him unless we are ready to show equal concern for others' needs, equal respect for everyone's human dignity, equal concern for the poor and equal respect for the excluded and the marginalised in society?

At Mass, we all receive in equal measure the Bread of Heaven, the Bread of Eternal Life. Can we worthily receive Holy Communion if, by anything we do or anything we fail to do, we are a cause of anyone's or any group's being denied their fair share of the bread of this world? In other words, can we sincerely say 'Amen', 'Yes', to his Body unless we also demand political programmes offering justice to all, and not just 'handouts' to the favoured groups? St Paul says:

> Anyone who eats the bread or drinks the Cup of the Lord unworthily will be behaving unworthily toward the Body and Blood of the Lord ... A person who eats and drinks [the Eucharist] without recognising the Body, is eating and drinking his own condemnation. (1 Cor 11:27-29)

He continues: 'Surely you have enough respect for the community of God not to make poor people embarrassed' (1 Cor 11:22).

Two kinds of 'recognition of the Body' are referred to here as conditions for worthy communion. First, we must recognise the bread and the Cup as 'truly and really and substantially' Christ's very Body and Christ's true Blood. Secondly, we must recognise the whole community and particularly the poor as equal parts of the Body of Christ, entitled to share in the respect which we have for Christ's Body in the Mass and entitled to share in the reverence and care which we show towards Christ's Body in Holy Communion.

There is a politics implied in the Mass. It is the politics of justice, the politics of love, the politics of compassion, the politics of respect for human rights and human dignity. This is the politics which St Paul implies when he says: 'Make sure that your citizenship is worthy of the Gospel of Christ' (Phil 1:27) – the word 'citizenship' here is the Greek word *politeusthe*, from which our word for politics comes.

LET US CALL TO MIND OUR SINS

By the standard of Christ's Gospel we all stand rebuked and condemned. We are all sinners against justice and against love. When we examine our consciences at the beginning of Mass or when we prepare for confession, we think readily of 'familiar' faults, perhaps based on lists we have used since childhood. We concentrate more on person-to-person relationships than on our duties in justice to others and to society. We think rather of personal faults than of our 'social sins'. Justice is the great 'no-go area' of most examinations of conscience. Justice is the great 'missing witness' from most confessions.

Despite a sad decline in the practice of confession in this country, many men and women in Ireland – young and old – will go to confession at Christmas and during Lent, and will receive Holy Communion at Christmas and Easter. We thank God for that grace. Christmas, Lent and Easter are wonderful occasions for looking deep into our consciences about justice – individual justice, group justice, social justice. Christmas, Lent or Easter would be an appropriate time for determining to amend our lives in the matter of justice, whether as individual workers, employers, managers, business people, professionals, traders, or as members of employers' organisations, trade unions, or professional groups.

We have sinned in the matter of justice. We have sinned by things we have done, and by things we have failed to do. But at Mass, where we confess together that we are all sinners, we ask one another to pray that the Lord our God may forgive us, for he is almighty and he demonstrates his almighty power most of all by showing pardon and pity.

The Lord, who is in our midst upon our altar, is the Lord who was betrayed, arrested, sentenced and mocked for us. He is the Lord who was given up in death for us so that our sins might be forgiven. He offers that atoning death for us as we gather round the altar, sinful and yet sorrowful, begging to be filled by him with every grace and blessing. He offers to the Father for us at Mass the prayer he prayed for us upon the Cross: 'Father, forgive them; they do not know what they are doing' (Lk 23:24). He is among us at Mass; he is with us in Holy Communion, as 'the Lamb of God who takes away the sins of the world'.

Our past, the past of our country, has much to regret and much to condemn, many missed opportunities, many wrong turnings. But God, who takes away our sins, is the God who 'makes all things new' (Rev 21:5). Because of his forgiveness 'the world of the past is gone' (Rev 21:4). Let us prepare to celebrate every Sunday, because every Sunday is 'resurrection day', by 'getting rid of all the old yeast of evil and wickedness, having only the unleavened bread of sincerity and truth' (1 Cor 5:7-8). We are God's holy people because we are God's forgiven people. We can go from Mass in peace, because Christ has forgiven us our sins.

Sunday Mass is Christ's healing of time past. It is Christ's grace and strength for the time to come. It is the beginning of a new week. Sunday Mass can transform the week's work, its decisions, its relationships, its standards. Sunday Mass calls us to a Christian way of working and deciding, and a Christian way of behaving towards our fellow human beings. Sunday Mass, every Mass, can be the beginning of a whole new way of existence in justice, love and peace.

Chapter 3

Eucharistic Devotion (I)

The supreme eucharistic devotion is the offering of Holy Mass; this chapter is, however, concerned with the worship of the Blessed Eucharist outside of Mass. Yet this way of describing it might suggest wrongly that such worship is unrelated to Mass itself or even inconsistent with it; I hope to show that the worship in question is both theologically and liturgically an extension of the celebration of Mass itself. To call the devotions I shall be discussing 'extra-liturgical eucharistic devotion' is equally inconsistent, because their roots are within the liturgical celebration of the Eucharist and their antecedents are found in very ancient strata of the eucharistic liturgy; also because fully developed forms of these devotions – such as the eucharistic procession and adoration of the reserved Blessed Sacrament – are found within the liturgy proper, especially that of Holy Week. The terminological problem, however, is relatively unimportant. Our subject matter is easily identifiable as including all forms of worship centring on the reserved Blessed Sacrament, 'Visits', Eucharistic Adoration, Benediction, Exposition, Processions and so on.

THE PERMANENT REAL PRESENCE
It is convenient to begin with a statement of the irrevocable commitment of the faith of the Church in this connection. The eucharistic dogmas of Trent cannot properly be described as being indicative of 'Counter-Reformation' hardening or narrowing of doctrine under Protestant pressure. Karl Rahner writes:

> Since the dogma of transubstantiation, even in its explicit formulations, has stood for centuries in the faith of the Church,

the Church would have had to deny its own being, as it understood itself to be, if it gave up this doctrine. While the Council of Trent had to struggle to find the correct expression for its faith in such matters as inherent righteousness, certainty of salvation, and so on, it was otherwise with transubstantiation. There was no real debate about it at the Council. The Council regarded this doctrine as something definitive, on which there could be no going back.[1]

The following are the Tridentine definitions most relevant to our theme:

> First of all, the Holy Council teaches, and openly and plainly professes, that after the consecration of bread and wine our Lord Jesus Christ, true God and true man, is truly, really and substantially contained in the august sacrament of the Holy Eucharist under the appearance of those sensible things. For there is no conflict in this that our Saviour sits always at the right hand of the Father in heaven according to the natural mode of existing, and yet is in many other places sacramentally present to us in his own substance by a manner of existence which, though we can scarcely express it in words, yet with our understanding illuminated by faith, we can conceive and ought most firmly to believe is possible to God ... The most Holy Eucharist has indeed this in common with the other sacraments that it is a symbol of a sacred thing and a visible form of an invisible grace; but there is found in it this excellent and peculiar characteristic that, whereas the other sacraments first have the

---

1   'The Presence of Christ in the Sacrament of the Lord's Supper' (in part the text of a lecture addressed to Protestant and Catholic theologians in 1958), *Theological Investigations,* IV (London: Darton, Longman and Todd, 1966), pp. 287–311, p. 297. Cf. p. 287: 'The doctrine of the real presence of Christ in the sacrament did not cause the Council Fathers much difficulty at Trent. They merely repeated, as was in itself the right thing to do, what the Church had already been saying for many hundreds of years before then when such discussion arose, in the same explicit formulas.'

power of sanctifying when one uses them, in the Eucharist there is the author himself of sanctity before it is used. For the apostles had not yet received the Eucharist from the hands of the Lord when he himself told them that what he was giving them was his own body ... There is, therefore, no room for doubt that all the faithful of Christ may, in accordance with a custom always received in the Catholic Church, give to his most holy sacrament in veneration the worship of *latria*, which is due to the true God. Neither is it to be less adored for the reason that it was instituted by Christ the Lord in order to be received. For we believe that in it the same God is present of whom the eternal Father, when introducing him to the world, says: 'And let all the angels of God adore him' (Heb 1:6); whom the Magi, falling down, adored (Mt 2:11); who, finally, as the Scriptures testify, was adored by the apostles in Galilee (Mt 28:17) ...

The Council goes on to express explicit approval of the particularly solemn veneration extended to the most holy sacrament on the feast of Corpus Christi and to the eucharistic processions associated with the feast. These, it says, are an appropriate celebration of the victory over death and the triumph of the divine Redeemer, which are made present in the Eucharist.

These positive statements of doctrine are followed by canons in which contrary teaching is condemned. Those relevant to our theme are the following:

If anyone shall say that after the consecration is completed the body and blood of our Lord Jesus Christ are not in the admirable sacrament of the Eucharist, but are there only *in usu*, while being taken, but not before or after, and that in the hosts or consecrated particles which are reserved or which remain after Communion, the true body of the Lord does not remain – *anathema sit* ...

If anyone shall say that in the holy sacrament of the Eucharist Christ, the only begotten Son of God, is not to be adored with the worship of *latria*, also outwardly manifested, and is consequently neither to be venerated with a special festive solemnity nor to be solemnly borne about in procession according to the laudable and universal rite and custom of holy church, or is not to be set publicly before the people to be adored and that the adorers thereof are adolaters – *anathema sit*.

If anyone shall say that it is not lawful that the Holy Eucharist be reserved in a sacred place, but immediately after consecration must necessarily be distributed among those present, or that it is not lawful that it be carried with honour to the sick – *anathema sit* ...[2]

Rahner comments on this Tridentine teaching:

It is actually plain heresy to say (in theory and hence also in practice) that Jesus Christ in the sacrament of the altar is not to be honoured with an external cult of adoration, that he is not to be celebrated in a special feast, that eucharistic processions and 'exposition' are to be rejected or that reservation of the sacrament on the altar is to be abandoned.[3]

Herbert McCabe, replying in the *Clergy Review* to criticism of his December 1964 article on 'The Real Presence', wrote:

My article on 'The Real Presence' was evidently unsatisfactory if only because fair-minded readers have the impression that it was 'trying to circumvent what has been defined by the Council of Trent'. Since conciliar definitions are part of the

---

2 *Sessio XIII, Decretum de SS. Eucharistia*, apud Denzinger-Bannwart-Rahner, p. 874, p. 876, pp. 878–9, p. 886, pp. 888–9.

3 'On Developing Eucharistic Devotion', *Mission and Grace* (London: Sheed and Ward, 1963), pp. 302–3.

data of theology, such an attempt would not be theology at all. Thus, for example, a denial of transubstantiation cannot form any part of Catholic theology.[4]

It is in liturgy and prayer that dogma finds its completion, just as it is in liturgy and prayer that dogma has one of its important sources and its setting in the Church's life. It is a striking thing that the language one uses to describe dogma is similar to the language one uses to describe sacrament. Karl Rahner, speaking of 'The Word and the Eucharist', writes:

> The *opus operatum* is the eschatologically unconditional word of God to man, which is no longer in the balance and in danger of being abrogated by a new and different word in the history of salvation. The *opus operatum* is the eschatologically efficacious word of God, as the absolute self-realisation of the Church, according to its essence as the primary sacrament ... [This] is clearly only possible where it is a matter of the whole Church's being committed to this truth. ... Each sacrament is an act of the absolute self-realisation of the Church as an absolute commitment ... [In the Eucharist] the Church realises itself in an absolute commitment which not merely regards the individual: the Church itself, as the community of salvation, actuates itself supremely in the sacrifice and meal of the Eucharist ... The efficacious word of the Mass, being the proclamation on the death of Christ, is the primary *kerygma* ...[5]

These terms have an obvious resemblance to the words already quoted about the dogma of transubstantiation:

---

4   *The Clergy Review* (March 1965), p. 233. The article in question was published in *The Clergy Review* (December 1964), pp. 749–59.

5   *Theological Investigations*, IV, pp. 274–5, p. 281, p. 286. Cf. Schillebeeckx, *Christ the Sacrament* (London: Sheed and Ward, 1963), pp. 119–20, pp. 126–7.

> Since the dogma of transubstantiation has stood for centuries in the faith of the Church, the Church would have had to deny its own being, as it understood itself to be, if it gave up this doctrine.[6]

Behind this rapprochement of words lies an important truth, which we need to grasp and affirm anew: that dogma is the Word of God present in the faith of the Church, and dogma is therefore a word of power, of liberty, of salvation, of life. To quote Rahner again:

> If the Church were not, by the triumphant grace of God, always the believing Church, it would not be the word which it is, triumphant, eschatological and efficacious, nor would it then be the word which is the triumphant eschatological presence of the Lord.[7]

Dogma is the assimilation by the believing, divinely sustained and guided ecclesial community of the Word of God. It is the Church's reading of Holy Scripture. Dogma is not an explanation of Scripture but a proclamation of it. Transubstantiation is frequently objected to as a presumptuous effort by human reason to explain the *how* of the real presence.[8] It is not. It is rather an obedient determination of the Church to take literally and affirm categorically the divine declaration of the *that* of the Real Presence. Transubstantiation affirms no more than Scripture, and no less. As Rahner puts it: 'The doctrine of transubstantiation tells me no more than the words of Christ, when I take them seriously.'

---

6   Op. cit., p. 297.
7   Op. cit., p. 285.
8   Professor Ian T. Ramsey, who became Bishop of Durham, quotes Lancelot Andrewes as replying to Cardinal Bellarmine: 'We believe no less than you that the presence is real. [But] concerning the *method* of the presence we define nothing rashly ...' Dr Ramsey recommends this attitude as respecting mystery and conducive to worship. These are precisely the merits of the Tridentine dogma, correctly understood. See Ian T. Ramsey, *Religious Language* (London: SCM Press, 1957), pp. 184–5.

The dogma, he says, is not an 'ontic explanation' of revealed truth, explaining it in terms of something else which would make its meaning clearer. It is rather a 'logical explanation', interpreting it in its own terms and therefore bound to the words of revelation and intelligible only in reference to the words of revelation.[9]

This is why dogma shares in the power of the revealed Word itself and is living and effectual like it. In few contexts is the dynamic quality of dogma more manifest than in that of eucharistic devotion, which Teilhard de Chardin refers to as 'The great highway opened up in the Church by the onrush of the cult of the Holy Eucharist.'[10]

The question has been raised as to whether transubstantiation is any longer an effective *shibboleth* of the specific belief of the Catholic Church in the Real Presence. It is certainly undeniable, especially in the light of the encyclical *Mysterium Fidei*, that no theological statement which modifies the Tridentine formula in such a way as to give it a meaning other than the original one intended by the Council, can be reconciled with Catholic faith. Any new terminology must respect and presuppose the truth affirmed by transubstantiation.[11]

This is not the immediate concern of this chapter, but I should be prepared to argue that willingness to adore and worship the reserved Blessed Sacrament is an unquestionable *shibboleth* of the specific Catholic faith in the Eucharist. I now turn to the sources and the theology of that worship.

ADORATION OF REAL PRESENCE IN THE EARLY CHURCH

To the assertion that devotions centred on the reserved Blessed Sacrament did not exist in the early Church, Karl Rahner wryly replies:

---

9   *Theological Investigations*, IV, pp. 300–4. Cf. Joseph M. Powers, *Eucharistic Theology* (London: Burns and Oates, 1968), p. 30, p. 117, pp. 140–4, p. 156.

10 *Le Milieu Divin* (London: Fontana Books, 1964), p. 123.

11 Pope Paul VI, *Mysterium Fidei*, pp. 23–5, pp. 46–7. See summary of the discussion in Powers, op. cit., pp. 111–54; and the author's conclusions, pp. 154–79. Compare Colman O'Neill, O.P., *New Approaches to the Eucharist* (Dublin: Gill, Logos, 1967), pp. 71–86.

Those who exalt the early centuries into an absolute standard
in matters of devotion ought to do it consistently (or abandon
it, as an absolute, altogether): which would mean applying it to
fasting, to a thorough-going preference and pre-eminence for
the virginal state over marriage, to the length of the liturgy, to
out-and-out monastic asceticism, and to many other things.

He insists that 'a practice with a thousand years of history behind it
has its rights, even if they are not the first thousand years.' He stresses
the place of development in the thought of the Church, and the
legitimacy of conclusions which have not always been explicit and
which yet, once given, become from then on part of the *permanent
self-fulfilment* of the Church.[12]

There is plenty of evidence in the early Church for the reverence
shown towards the eucharistic species preserved after Mass and
carried home for the purpose of communion. Tertullian, St Cyprian,
Novatian, Origen, St Ambrose, St Jerome, St Augustine, the Apostolic
Constitutions, St Basil and St Cyril of Alexandria are formal on this
point. The Irish Columbanan monks introduced the custom of carrying
the Blessed Sacrament with them on their voyages, in a receptacle called
a 'chrismal'. They called it 'the sacrifice' and treated it with extreme
reverence. The seventh-century penitentials impose drastic penalties
for any negligence or irreverence towards the sacred species. St Sirin,
Bishop of Corchester in the seventh century, had the habit of carrying
the Blessed Sacrament suspended in a pyx or *palla* round his neck,
placing it on the altar while celebrating Mass.[13] There is archaeological
evidence of reservation of the Blessed Sacrament, even of the custom
of keeping a lamp lit before it, from the earliest centuries.[14]

What is important to notice is that this is not so much a matter
of adding new extra-liturgical devotions to the eucharistic liturgy

12 *Mission and Grace*, I, pp. 304–5.
13 See Cabriel Comment, 'Adoration Eucharistique et renouveau liturgique', *Parole et Pain*, 13, April 1966, pp. 89–92. Cf. *Mysterium Fidei*, pp. 56–61.
14 *Parole et Pain*, loc. cit., p. 92.

48

than of developing and expressing more explicitly the faith and adoration already inherent in the liturgy itself. The Anglican theologian, Dr Eric Mascall, in his remarkable book *Corpus Christi*, restated a thesis of Dom Gregory Dix in these words:

> The crucial moment in the development of eucharistic piety comes not with the emergence of extra-liturgical devotions in the late Middle Ages but with the emergence of intra-liturgical devotion to our Lord about the end of the fifth century.

This itself, he hastens to add, was not an innovation but an explicitation of a belief in the reality of the eucharistic presence which was there in the Church from the beginning.[15] St Augustine prescribes: 'Let no one eat the flesh of Jesus Christ without having first adored it ... Not only do we not sin in thus adoring it, but we would sin if we did not do so.'[16] Prayers addressed to Christ, present in the Eucharist, such as the *Agnus Dei*, are found in the eucharistic liturgy from the seventh century.

The fact that eucharistic devotion grows from within the eucharistic liturgy is theologically very significant. It is many years since Vonier and de la Taille stressed the importance of seeing eucharistic devotion as the extension of the moment of the eucharistic celebration which lies between the Consecration and the Communion, and drew upon this insight to lay the foundations of a far-reaching renewal of theology of eucharistic devotion.[17]

A SACRAMENTAL PRESENCE

Indeed, the renewal of the theology of the eucharistic sacrifice, in which these two men were the great pioneers, had important

---

15 E.L. Mascall, *Corpus Christi* (London: Longman, 1965), p. 259.

16 In Ps 98:9; P.L. 37, col. 1767; cited in *Mysterium Fidei*, p. 55.

17 Dom A. Vonier, 'The Relationship between Mass and Benediction, and Prayers before the Blessed Sacrament Exposed', *Sketches and Studies in Theology* (London: Burns, Oates and Washbourne, 1940), pp. 107–45; de la Taille, 'The Real Presence and its Sacramental Function', op. cit., pp. 201–17.

repercussions for the theology of the reserved sacrament. Both men exposed the falsehood of a tendency, not uncommon in theology since the sixteenth century, to seek the explanation of the sacrificial character of the Mass in a real and distinct immolation of Christ endured in the conditions of the eucharistic presence itself, and consisting in his suffering of abasement and humiliation through the fact of transubstantiation.[18]

This theory of the eucharistic sacrifice had as a consequence, in some forms of eucharistic devotion and some pious writing about the Eucharist, a tendency to view Christ in the Blessed Sacrament as 'the divine prisoner in the tabernacle', to speak of his loneliness in empty or closed churches or throughout the night hours. Vonier and de la Taille vigorously combated such notions as theologically aberrant and spiritually unsound. Vonier declared:

> We cannot allow on any account that the person of Christ, the soul of Christ, the heart of Christ in the Eucharist can be under any shadow of suffering or sadness. This would be to deny the dogma that says that Christ sits at the right hand of the Father. If there is in many a manual of piety, language that cannot be interpreted otherwise than as a compassion for a Christ who is actually suffering in the Eucharist, let such passages be purgated without remorse; they endanger the faith of Catholics in the mystery of Christ's glorification.

He goes on to say that there is, of course, a place for compassion and reparation in eucharistic devotion, but it is compassion for the sufferings of his mortal life and the foreseen sins of all the ages, including profanations or neglect of the Blessed Eucharist, which caused those sufferings. But Christ's sacramental state as such is not

---

18 Vonier, 'Eucharistic Theology', *Sketches and Studies in Theology*, pp. 86–9; cf. op. cit., pp. 140–5; 'Key to the Doctrine of the Eucharist', *Collected Works II* (London: Burns and Oates, 1952), pp. 270–4; de la Taille, *Mysterium Fidei* (Paris: Beauchesne, 1924), pp. 295–301, pp. 306–16.

a state or a cause of new suffering for Christ: 'The Son of God is no more humbled through transubstantiation than the Holy Ghost is humbled through dwelling in the soul of a man.'[19]

Vonier lays down the general principle that any form of eucharistic devotion is sound so long as it respects 'the sacramental conditions and the sacrificial aspect' of the presence of Christ in the Eucharist. Eucharistic devotion must, in other words, always remember that Christ is really present in his risen and glorified person, as he is now in heaven, but that he is present, not in the natural condition in which his body now exists in heaven, but sacramentally. And he is present as the victim of sacrifice, to be received by us in communion of that life of oneness with the Father which he secured for us by his sacrifice.[20] Vonier emphasises his point by saying:

> If we were met by Christ in person in our churches, such gracious encounters would have nothing in common with what is called the sacramental presence. His presence in the sacrament must be truly such that at no time could it be seen otherwise than by the eye of faith. One is justified in saying that it is the very condition of the sacramental presence to transcend all vision and all experience, even of the highest order, because there is really no kind of perceptive power in man, or even in angel, capable of reacting to that state of being which is proper to the sacrament.[21]

It is worth noting that Vonier's eucharistic theology, with all its striking relevance to contemporary discussion, is entirely based on St Thomas Aquinas. In the context in question, Vonier quotes

---

19 *Sketches and Studies in Theology*, pp. 141–4.
20 Op. cit., p. 109, p. 126.
21 *Key to the Doctrine of the Eucharist*, p. 244. Elsewhere he writes: 'To state the Eucharist in phrases which can only be true in Christ's natural life, is to relinquish a whole new world of divine revelation' (op. cit., p. 247).

Aquinas as arguing that even an angel could see the body of Christ 'according to the mode of being which it has in this sacrament' only in the vision of the divine essence and not by connatural angelic intelligence.[22] We may recall too that Aquinas himself is adamant that eucharistic miracles and apparitions are not a perceiving of Christ in his natural form. In this, he is present and visible only in heaven.[23]

However strong the psychological power of an apparition or miracle to corroborate a dogma, they could never, in the absolute sense, confirm the dogma. We would always be more sure of the truth of the dogma than we are of the reality of the preternatural occurrence. For the former, we have divine authority, for the latter, only human credibility.[24] The net result of Aquinas's discussions on how Christ exists and whether he can be seen in the Eucharist is that his presence is of an utterly unique, sacramental kind, reducible to no other form of presence and knowable only by faith.

A SACRIFICIAL AND COMMUNIONAL PRESENCE

The truth that Christ's presence in the Eucharist is simply a prolongation of the sacrament-sacrifice of the Eucharist, entails that authentic eucharistic devotion shall be a prayerful participation in the sacrifice and a preparation for Communion. Contemporary discussion often emphasises that Christ is present in the Eucharist precisely as food to be received. Father Schoonenberg remarks that 'Christ comes, not to be enthroned in the host, but to live in our heart.'[25] The observation is not new. De la Taille pointed out that Christ might conceivably have chosen other elements to transubstantiate into his body – such as precious stones or precious metals – if his only purpose had been to ensure his presence in material proximity to men. Instead, he chose food: something to be received

22 Op. cit., p. 245; the reference is to *S. Theol.*, p. 3767.
23 *S. Theol.*, p. 3768.
24 See C.B. Daly, 'The Meaning of Lourdes', in *Mother of the Redeemer*, ed. K. McNamara (Dublin: Gill, 1959), p. 255.
25 Cited by Colman O'Neill, op. cit., p. 58.

into our very being as a sign that the presence of his body is a means of 'spiritual union by which I form but one spirit with the Lord'.[26]

Much before de la Taille, someone who learned about the Blessed Eucharist, not from theology books, but from the catechism, the New Testament, the Imitation, and prayer, St Thérèse of Lisieux, said this:

> It is not to remain in a golden ciborium that Christ comes down each day from heaven, but to find another heaven, far dearer to him than the first, the heaven of our soul, made in his image, the living temple of the adorable Trinity.[27]

The sacrificial reference of eucharistic devotion was preserved in many patterns of prayers of adoration, such as the modelling of holy hours on the four-fold purposes of adoration, reparation, thanksgiving, petition, or the practice of 'visits' of uniting oneself with all the Masses being offered up throughout the world. The communional reference was respected by the almost universal practice of terminating a 'visit' or a holy hour by an 'act of spiritual communion'. But there is no point in claiming that the new insights of Vonier and de la Taille, and of more recent theologians of the Eucharist, have entered as fully as they might have into the mentalities of either priests or people, or have influenced as salutarily as they should have our modes of eucharistic devotion.

THE CONTEMPORARY CRISIS

For there is no blinkering the fact that there has been, throughout much of the Catholic world, a marked decline in extra-liturgical eucharistic prayer, and indeed in personal and contemplative prayer generally, in recent years. This is due in part to the tremendous improvement in the quality of our liturgical prayer; and this is surely one of the greatest graces the Council brought to the Church. But

---

26 *Mystery of Faith and Human Opinion*, p. 214.
27 *Manuscrits Autobiographiques* (Carmel de Lisieux, 1957), p. 117.

there are other, less reassuring causes, such as semantic and theological confusion about the significance of the rediscovery of earthly values and of Christian commitment to the secular city, with consequent doubt as to the relevance or even validity of contemplative prayer.

Authoritative voices have warned for many decades about the dangers of such a decline for the life and mission of the Church, for the state of theology and for the future of the liturgical movement itself. Henri de Lubac, in *Corpus Mysticum*, wrote:

> It is not the human fact of meeting together to celebrate the Christian mysteries in common, it is not the collective exaltation that a suitable preparation can produce on such occasions, which will ever realise the unity of the members of Christ. There will be no such unity without the forgiveness of sins, first fruit of the outpoured blood, without memorial of the Passion, offering to the heavenly Father, conversion of heart – these are the realities, and they are all of them interior realities – without which we will never have anything but a caricature of the Christian community we seek. But it is no human mirage which the Eucharist offers us: it is a mystery of faith. It is the whole mystery of salvation, which must be mediated ...[28]

It was very early in the history of the modern liturgical revival that Romano Guardini warned of the harm that could be done to the liturgy itself by the neglect of its contemplative aspect. Contact with the supratemporal, the eternal, would be lost. The faithful would make their home in time, not eternity. Religion would conform itself more and more to the world, would become little more than a consecration of earthly existence – a sort of sanctification of human activity.[29] Hans Urs von Balthasar described in these terms the consequence of divorcing liturgy from contemplation:

---

28 *Corpus Mysticum* (Paris: Aubier, 1948), pp. 293–4.
29 *L'Esprit de la Liturgie*, translated from the German text of 1918 (Paris: Plon, 1930), p. 267.

Either the sacramental principle is pushed to extremes and has a quasi-magical power attributed to it; or else mundane activities are held exaggeratedly sacred, and a kind of theology of the things of earth set up which ascribes to business, technology, material well-being, the state and secular culture, an over-riding place among the factors which build up and further the kingdom of God – this view is currently held nowadays precisely where contemplation is under-valued ... A liturgical movement unaccompanied by a contemplative is a kind of romanticism, an escape from time, and inevitably calls up, by opposition, the counter-romanticism of a false conception of the sacred character of secular activity.[30]

It is therefore a matter of pastoral urgency to revalorise and renew eucharistic devotion and the contemplative prayer which is its normal expression. And the condition for this is to impart a correct liturgical and theological sense to this devotion. It was again Father de Lubac who said that modern developments in eucharistic piety

tended to move in the direction of a too individualistic devotion and were poorly defended against sentimental excesses. The result was that one of the most magnificent instances of progress to be found in the whole history of Christianity was prevented from realising some of its best fruits.[31]

MASS HELD IN MEDITATION
I have already referred to the phrase 'the Mass held in meditation'. The most obvious need for meditative eucharistic prayer is a psychological one: it is impossible, during the brief duration of the eucharistic action itself, to have anything like an adequate realisation of the mystery which is being enacted and therefore to achieve

---

30 *Prayer*, translated by A.V. Littledale (London: Chapman, 1961), p. 98.
31 *Corpus Mysticum*, pp. 291–2.

anything like an adequate participation in its mystical movement. The Mass must be prepared in prayer, prolonged in prayer, assimilated through lifelong prayer, if it is to be for us authentically the Mass. The natural focus for this prayer is the reserved host itself, perpetuated presence of the sacrifice, living source of grace and magnetic pole of charity and unity, permanent promise of communion with the Father in the Son. The Holy Eucharist is the concentrate of the whole of Christian reality, the supreme manifestation of what the Church believes and is. Rahner writes:

> The Eucharist is 'word': because here the incarnate *Logos* of God is himself present in his substance; because here the absolute proclamation of the whole mystery of salvation takes place: there is the anamnesis, in which the event of God's giving himself to the world and the acceptance of this gift on the Cross of the Son becomes actually present amongst us, sacramentally, in the space and time we live in; and there is the anticipation, sacramentally, of final salvation in the *pignus futurae gloriae*, because here the *death* of Christ and his coming are exhibited and proclaimed; and because here we have the supreme self-realisation of the Church.[32]

Rahner and Häussling declare: 'Nowhere is everything which the Church is and has the mission to announce more intensely manifested than in the celebration of the Eucharist.'[33]

In the Mass, the infinity of divine love meets the totality of human experience in order to absorb it into the eternal life of the Blessed Trinity. A lifetime of eucharistic meditation would be too little to explore the meaning and develop the personal, social and cosmic implication of this mystery.

---

32 *Theological Investigations*, IV, p. 281.
33 Karl Rahner and Angelus Häussling, *The Celebration of the Eucharist* (London: Burns, Oates and Herder, 1968), p. 93.

Chapter 4

Eucharistic Devotion (II)

EUCHARIST AND MYSTICISM

A still more profound reason for eucharistic meditation is provided by the revealed theology of the Eucharist, as we find this particularly in St John's Gospel. The sixth chapter of St John's Gospel presents the promise of the Eucharist in a profoundly mystical setting. The language recalls the Sapiential Books of the Old Testament, where divine Wisdom invites people to a banquet in which Wisdom herself is eaten and assimilated by her guests. Parallels are obvious with the Book of Proverbs and with the Book of Sirach:

> Whoever is ignorant let him step this way.
> To the fool [Wisdom] says:
> Come and eat my bread,
> drink the wine I have prepared!
> Leave your folly and you will live,
> walk in the ways of understanding. (Prv 9:4-6)

> They who eat me will hunger for more.
> They who drink me will thirst for more.
> Whoever listens to me will never have to blush
> whoever acts as I dictate will never sin.[1]

---

1 Ecclesiasticus 24:29-30. Compare Baruch 3:8-5, 9; Isaiah 55:1-3. For this parallelism, see A. Feuillet, *Le Discours sur le pain de vie*, Foi Vivante (Paris: Desclée de Brouwer, 1967), pp. 39–87. See also Congar, 'Les deux formes de pain', *Sacerdoce et laïcat* (Paris: Cerf, 1962), pp. 123–59; Rahner, 'The Word and the Eucharist', *Theological Investigations*, IV, pp. 253–86.

Jesus, in the sixth chapter of St John, is revealing that he is in his person the Incarnate Wisdom of God, and that union with his person, through meditative assimilation of his word and sacramental eating of his flesh and blood, is the final fulfilment of man's endless hunger to possess and be possessed by divine wisdom.

It seems idle to analyse the chapter into a mystical section concerned with Christ's word and a sacramental section concerned with Christ's eucharistic body. The mystical section is eucharistic and the eucharistic section is mystical. Word and Eucharist, faith and sacrament, mysticism and liturgy are inseparable for St John, as they have been throughout the great Catholic tradition. We are, in St John's sixth chapter, at the source of the theological tradition which defines sacrament as *visibile verbum*; which declares *accedit verbum ad elementum et fit sacramentum*; which calls the sacraments *signa protestantis fidem*. We are also, of course, at the source of the primordial Christian tradition which refused to separate the liturgy of the Word from the liturgy of the Eucharist, and which familiarly spoke of the table of the Word of God as inseparable from the table of the body and blood of Christ. In early Romanesque mosaics and in the ninth-century evangelaries, we find Christ represented as supreme bishop of the Church, presiding over the eucharistic celebration, holding a host in one hand and the Bible in the other.[2]

A closely related theme in St John's sixth chapter is that of discipleship. The chapter must be read in conjunction with the discourse on 'The Vine and the Branches', which is itself undeniably eucharistic in meaning, and indeed with the whole corpus of pre-Passion discourses of Our Lord in chapters 12–17. The disciple is the one who has completely assimilated Christ's word of truth and has, through loving union with Christ's person, become completely identified with Christ and thus incorporated into his filial relationship with the Father:

---

2   See Congar, op. cit., p. 151.

If you remain in me and my words remain in you, you may ask what you will and you shall get it. It is to the glory of my Father that you should bear much fruit, and then you will be really my disciples. As the Father has loved me so I have loved you. If you keep my commandments you will remain in my love just as I have kept my Father's commandments and remain in his love. (Jn 15:7-11)

I have made your name known to the men you took from the world to give to me … Now at last they know that all that you have given me comes indeed from you, for I have given them the teaching you gave to me and they have truly accepted this, that I came from you, and they have believed that it was you who sent me … Father, righteous One, the world has not known you, but I have known you, and these have known that you have sent me. I have made your name known to them and will continue to make it known, so that the love with which you loved me may be in them and so that I may be in them. (Jn 17:6-9, 25-6)

Here we have the divinely revealed source of all eucharistic contemplation. For these chapters are eucharistic theology turned into prayer, Paschal Mystery spelled out by Christ himself in meditation. There is nothing in the rich new theological and liturgical thinking on the Paschal Mystery, nothing in the new insights into the Eucharist as the Pasch of the Church, which is not already contained in St John's Gospel. And this itself reveals an extraordinary identity with the apparently so much less mystical paschal message of the Synoptics and the apparently so personal paschal theology of St Paul.

Christ is our place of meeting with the Father, the point of merging between the descending movement of the Father's love towards us in Christ and the movement of our paschal return towards the Father in Christ. The risen body of Christ is the journey already completed, the union of humanity with God in principle consummated. It is this risen body which is present in the Eucharist and in the Church. To abide in Christ by prayerful union, to abide in the Church by loving discipleship, to abide in Christ by faith-filled reception of the Eucharist, these for St John's Gospel are inseparable from one another and are equivalent to abiding with Christ in the very love with which he, the Son, loves the Father and is loved by the Father.[3]

Let it be noted too that this mystical dimension of the Eucharist is no other-worldly escapism. It is striking that, just as no sacred writer emphasises more than St John the vertical-mystical aspect of the Blessed Eucharist, so too no New Testament writer stresses more than he its horizontal-social aspect:

> What we have seen and heard we are telling you so that you too may be in union with us as we are in union with the Father and with his Son Jesus Christ ... If we say that we are in union with God while we are living in darkness, we are lying because we are not living the truth. But if we live our lives in the light as he is in the light, we are in union with one another and the blood of Jesus, his Son, purifies us from all sin ... We have passed out of death and into life and of this we can be sure because we love our brothers. If you refuse to love, you must remain dead. To hate your brother is to be a murderer, and murderers, as you know, do not have eternal life in them. This has taught us love – that he gave up his life for us; and we, too, ought to give up our lives for our brothers (1 Jn 1:3, 6-7; 3:14-16).

We can see the same phenomenon of concern for humanity flowing from mystical absorption in God in three great modern Christians, whom it is right to call eucharistic mystics. St Thérèse of

---

3   See J.M.R. Tillard, *L'Eucharistie, Pâque de l'Eglise* (Paris: Cerf, 1964), pp. 15–50.

Lisieux, a Johannine saint if ever there were one, shows her mystical daring in making her own the words which Christ addressed to his Father in his great sacerdotal prayer, interpreting them in terms of a mission to intensify holiness in the Church – especially among priests – and to spread the love of Christ beyond every river of the globe.[4] Contemplative fusion of her soul with Christ's in Mass and Communion was accompanied by missionary longing to use Christ's eucharistic blood to purify and consecrate the earth.[5]

In his devotion to the Eucharist, Teilhard de Chardin found the inspiration for his passion to Christianise science and technology and human progress, to humanise and Christianise the cosmos and to unify mankind in Christ. He describes in the third person, though they are undoubtedly autobiographical, two mystical experiences related to the Blessed Eucharist, one entitled 'The Monstrance', one 'The Pyx'. In the first, the sacred host, as he gazes on it, seems to merge with the universe in an incandescence of fire and love. The world itself becomes an immense host, the cosmos finding its supreme fulfilment in a great act of love, in which all the capacities of love in the universe are purified and amalgamated in Christ, only evil remaining outside the circle of radiance, illuminating fitfully the surrounding darkness with a perverted glow.[6]

In the second experience, Teilhard, near the Front during World War I, is carrying the sacred species in a pyx and is seized with longing to be one completely with the eucharistic Lord, but at the same time filled with the conviction that this union cannot be complete until his life and work are fully eucharistified.

> I was separated from the host which I held in my hands by all the depth and all the surface of the years left to me to live and to divinise.[7]

---

4   *Manuscrits autobiographiques*, pp. 307–12.
5   Op. cit., p. 77, pp. 83–6, pp. 109–11, pp. 226–30.
6   'L'Ostensoir', *Hymne de l'Univers* (Paris: Seuil, 1961), pp. 77–81.
7   'La Custode', op. cit., pp. 85–92.

It should be noted that Teilhard's eucharistic piety was of the most orthodox kind. It was here that his notion of the *consecration mundi*, the Christification of the cosmos, was born.[8]

Authentic eucharistic mysticism is thus dynamic, cosmic, missionary. It is true, as Claudel puts it, addressing Rimbaud:

> What you looked for so far afield, eternity, is here is this life, perceptible to all the senses, lift your eyes, look, it's there, there in front of you, can't you see it, the azyme in the monstrance … What you looked for so far afield, beyond the forest, across the sea and on the other side of the islands, your mother and sister know it all the time, without ever having to budge from Charleville.[9]

And yet Rimbaud could come to the Eucharist only by bringing to it his wanderings and filling with it the depth and the surface of his tortured years. To voyage to the discovery of Sacraments can be one fruit of eucharistic devotion. The Blessed Sacrament in their 'chrismal' made it impossible for Irish monks to stay in their Charlevilles and drove them out across seas and forests to carry the incandescence of the host into the dark places of a barbarous Europe.

MEMORIAL, PRAISE COMMUNION

The moments of eucharistic prayer should reflect the moments of eucharistic celebration. St Thomas has classically formulated these as recall of the memory of Christ's Passion, made present again in the Eucharist; reception of his body in Holy Communion; penetration of our personalities by his grace; anticipation of final union with Christ in the glory of the Father. About all of these, modern movements of renewal in the Church have given us rich new insights.

---

8   See H. de Lubac, *La Prière du Pere Teilhard de Chardin* (Paris: Fayard, 1964), pp. 66–71.

9   'Consécration', *La Messe là-bas, Oeuvre poétique* (Paris: La Pléiade, 1957), pp. 501–2.

Recall of the memory of Christ's Passion is at the same time recall of the whole of God's mighty works in creation and salvation, in history and the Church. It is the Christian form of the great Jewish Berakah, the Prayer of the Passover, the prayer Christ himself must have prayed at the Last Supper. In Christ at last it is fulfilled. In him humanity has at last passed over from mortality to divine life, from earth to heaven. We thank God with the thanks of his Son. We reach God in the Passover of his Son.

The Jewish Berakah presupposed that the saving events recalled were also made present in the meal recalling them. Our Eucharist is not only salvation recalled but salvation effected by the very author of salvation himself made present, as Trent puts it. The sacrifice is communion of life with the Father in Christ who is oneness of life with the Father, whose risen body – now become spirit and life in the Father – is spirit-filling and life-giving in us. St Thomas said that the Eucharist is 'the consummation of spiritual life and the end of all the sacraments'.[10] It not only unites with Christ, it is Christ. It not only gives a share in the life of God, it is God's shared life in Christ.

Nothing can adequately express the praise and thanks we owe for this gift except the gift itself. But the gift can be given back only if we ourselves are totally given with it, and our lives and our work and our world as well. The world must be merged in our host and our Mass meditatively offered on the world if eucharistic adoration is to correspond with its object. The salvation-historic and the cosmic psalms are *berakoth* – this is why the psalms have always been held by the Church as her preferred prayer before the Eucharist. There is an unerring biblical and theological soundness about St Thomas' Eucharistic Offices. Their use of Bible readings and psalms could scarcely be improved by the best modern exegete or liturgist. Their prayers express the most sober and accurate eucharistic theology. Their use by the Church in her various eucharistic devotions should have been enough to provide a model for private eucharistic prayer.

---

10 *S. Theol.*, p. 3733.

BREAD OF LIFE: REFLECTIONS ON THE EUCHARIST

EUCHARIST AND ESCHATOLOGY

The writings of the great Lutheran scholar, Professor Joachim Jeremias, have uncovered new aspects of the recall of the memory of the Passion. Christ commanded his followers to repeat his sacrifice-meal in memory of him. Jeremias has convincingly argued that the phrase means 'in order that God may remember me'. The Eucharist is to be offered in order that God may continually remember his Son's sacrifice and bring it to its final and total consummation by ushering in the final judgement, by establishing the kingdom in the victorious power of its eschatological completeness, by bringing salvation to its climax in the parousia:

> This means that the death of the Lord is not proclaimed at every celebration of the meal as a past event but as an eschatological event, as the beginning of the New Covenant. The proclamation of the death of Jesus is not therefore intended to call to the remembrance of the community the event of the Passion; rather this proclamation expresses the vicarious death of Jesus as the beginning of the salvation time and prays for the coming of the consummation. As often as the death of the Lord is proclaimed at the Lord's supper and the *Maranatha* rises upwards, God is reminded of the unfulfilled climax of the work of salvation 'until [the goal is reached that] he comes'. Paul has therefore understood the *anamnesis* as the eschatological remembrance of God that is to be realised in the parousia.[11]

The eschatological longing thus inherent in the Eucharist is the opposite of a death wish; it is a life wish. It is the desire of Christ, perpetuated in his Church, that men may have life and may have it more abundantly. It is a prayer that sin, evil and error, death and hate may pass, so that holiness and truth, life and love may come.

---

11   N. Perris, trs., *The Eucharistic Words of Jesus* (London: SCM Press, 1966), pp. 253–4.

If we pray that the world pass, it is so that grace may come. The Eucharistic Prayer in the *Didache* ended thus:

> O Lord, remember thy Church, to free her from evil and perfect her in thy love. Sanctify her and gather her in from the four winds into the kingdom thou hast prepared for her ... May grace come and this world pass ... *Maranatha.* Amen.[12]

The eschatological kingdom is already begun in time in the eschatological community of the Church. To pray for the eschatological consummation is therefore to pray for the unity, charity, holiness, faith and missionary expansion of the Church. The eschatological kingdom includes the transformation of the world of matter itself into the new heaven and the new earth of the new creation. Prayer before the Blessed Sacrament cannot but be marked with this twofold passion, to sanctify and to spread the Church and to transform and Christify and eucharistify the earth. We can never forget, before the tabernacle, that Christ in the Eucharist is he 'who came to cast fire on earth and who desires nothing more than that it be enkindled'. We must always remember that Christ in the Eucharist is the resurrection already realised, the new heaven and the new earth already inaugurated. The French Scripture scholar, Benoit, writes summarising the doctrine of St Paul:

> In Christ, the cosmic renewal which is to characterise the eschatological era is already effected. The risen body of Jesus is the first cell of the new cosmos. In him the Spirit has already taken possession of matter, as he will one day take possession of the entire creation, at the parousia, when Christ will definitively recapitulate all things in himself. The bodies of Christ's faithful are already united to his body by the mystical union of Baptism and the Eucharist. With him they have risen from the dead.

---

12   Apud M.J. Rouet de Journel, *Enchiridion Partisicum* (Barcelona: Herder, 1946), n. 7.

What is for him a physical and definitive state is for them a mystical state which still awaits its consummation, but is no less real for all that.[13]

Nothing should have more attraction for modern thought, more impetus for modern action than eucharistic devotion. Blondel writes:

> I scarcely think of you, O God, except under the sweet form of Communion. Everything is there. It is the New and Eternal Covenant. It is the consummation of all your mighty deeds. It is the mystery of mysteries. It is the all of man, the end of the universe, the inauguration of eternity. Everything is there. Calvary with Nazareth and Bethlehem; the altar and the tabernacle, where your dwelling is permanent ... the tomb where you died and the heaven where we rise in glory.[14]

Teilhard de Chardin, in *Le milieu divin*, writes:

> From the beginning of the messianic preparation, up till the parousia, passing through the historic manifestation of Jesus and the phases of growth of his Church, a single event has been developing in the world; the Incarnation, realised in each individual, through the Eucharist.
> All the communions of a lifetime are one communion.
> All the communions of all men now living are one communion.
> All the communions of all men, present, past and future, are one communion.
> Grant, O God, that when I draw near to the altar to communion, I may henceforth discern the infinite perspectives hidden beneath the smallness and the nearness of the host in which

---

13 P. Benoit, 'L'Ascension', *Exégèse et théologie*, I (Paris: Cerf, 1961), p. 386.
14 *Carnets intimes*, I, p. 328.

you are concealed. I have already accustomed myself to seeing, beneath the stillness of that piece of bread, a devouring power which, in the words of the greatest doctors of your Church, far from being consumed by me, consumes me. Give me the strength to rise above the remaining illusions which tend to make me think of your touch as circumscribed and momentary. I am beginning to understand; under the sacramental species it is primarily through the 'accidents' of matter that you touch me, but, as a consequence, it is also through the whole universe in proportion as it ebbs and flows over me under your primary influence. In a true sense the arms and the heart which you open to me are nothing less than all the united powers of the world which, penetrated and permeated to their depths by your will, your tastes and your temperament, converge upon my being to form it, nourish it and bear it along towards the centre of your fire. In the host it is my life that you are offering me, O Jesus.

What can I do to gather up and answer that universal and enveloping embrace? *Quomodo comprehendam ut comprehensus sim?* To the total offer that is made me, I can only answer by a total acceptance. I shall therefore react to the eucharistic contact with the entire effort of my life – of my life of today and of my life of tomorrow, of my personal life and of my life as linked to all other lives. Periodically, the sacred species may perhaps fade away in me. But each time they will leave me a little more deeply engulfed in the layers of your omnipresence: living and dying, I shall never at any moment cease to move forward in you. Thus the precept implicit in your Church, that we must communicate everywhere and always, is justified with extraordinary force and precision. The Eucharist must invade my life. My life must become, as a result of the sacrament, an unlimited and endless contact with you – that life which seemed, a few moments ago, like a baptism with you in the waters of the world, reveals itself to me as communion with you through the world. It is the sacrament of life. The sacrament of my life – of my life received, of my life lived, of my life surrendered … Disperse, O Jesus, the clouds with your lightning! Show yourself to us as the mighty, the radiant, the risen! Come to us once again as the Pantocrator who filled the solitude of the cupolas in the ancient basilicas! Nothing less than this parousia is needed to counter-balance and dominate in our hearts the glory of the world that is coming into view. And so that we should triumph over the world with you, come to us clothed in the glory of the world.[15]

THROUGH DEATH TO LIFE

But the Eucharist keeps before our minds the true meaning of eschatology and prevents us from confounding it with temporal millenarism or socio-political messianism. The Eucharist reminds us that resurrection lies on the other side of death, and that Christian eschatology requires a radical break with merely human history. Christ's kingdom is not of this world. Christ had to suffer, had to be obedient even to death, in order to enter into his glory. We must bring to Christ for transformation through his death all that is un-Christed in our world. The glory of which we receive the pledge and foretaste in the Eucharist is ours only in so far as we do so.

Karl Rahner, in suggestive pages on the Eucharist as 'Sacrament of the Everyday', shows how Christ's death is the concentrate of all that is slow dying in our daily lives, all that is frailty, failure, banality, insecurity, solitude, pain and illness. All this Christ saw in the cup of the Last Supper, in the cup of the Garden of Gethsemane; all this he drank to the repulsive dregs on the Cross. In the Eucharist, we receive the dying of Christ for the transmutation of our daily dying, and it is this dying of ours which is taken hold of by the

---

15 *Le Milieu divin*, p. 124, pp. 126–7, p. 128.

Spirit of the risen Christ and permeated daily by the glory of the
new creation. The Eucharist is the means of gradual replacement
of our life-unto-death by the death-unto-life of Christ, but on
the condition of our suffering with him so that we may also rise
with him. Every Communion represents a profession of faith in the
Cross of the Lord.[16]

Rahner's sombre pages provide an important pendant to the
more optimistic pages of Teilhard already quoted. But both must
find their place in a full Christian synthesis, as both should find
expression in a balanced eucharistic piety.

THE EUCHARIST AND UNITY IN THE CHURCH

A theme which can never be absent from eucharistic prayer is
longing and intercession for even greater unity within the Church.
The Eucharist is the great protestation by Christ's disciples of their
love for one another in obedience to Christ's new commandment
and in remembrance of his condition for discipleship: 'By this love
you have for one another everyone will know that you are my
disciples' (Jn 13:34-35).

St Paul already sees in the eucharistic elements a symbol of the
unity of the Church. 'You are one bread, one body, all who partake
of the one bread.' The Eucharistic Prayer in the *Didache* contains
the words:

As this bread which we break was once scattered over the
hills and was gathered together to make one loaf, so may your
Church be gathered together from the ends of the earth into
one unity and so be admitted into your Kingdom.[17]

St Augustine powerfully develops the theme of Christ's ecclesial
body as the extension of his eucharistic body, and of the effect of

---

16 C. Moeller, trs., 'Sacrament du Quotidien', *L'Eucharistie et les hommes d'aujourdhui* (Paris:
Mame, 1965), pp. 169–94.
17 Apud Rouet de Journel, op. cit., n. 6.

the Eucharist as being the building up in charity and unity of the Church.

Father de Lubac has shown how the term *Corpus Mysticum* was first used of the eucharistic body of Christ before being applied to the Church. When the words *Corpus Christi* were used without qualification in the first eleven centuries, they referred to the Church – so strong was the conviction of the ecclesial reference of the Eucharist, so realist the understanding of the sense in which the Church was called the body of Christ.

St Thomas Aquinas untiringly stresses the ecclesial finality of the Eucharist. The effect of the sacrament, the *res et sacramentum*, is the building up of perfect charity and unity in the earthly Church, so as to bring it more and more into the pattern of the heavenly Church towards which it is in pilgrimage. Final identification of the Church on earth with the Church in heaven is the ultimate eschatological goal and the consummated effect of the Eucharist.

There is little doubt that when St Paul castigates the Corinthians for receiving Holy Communion unworthily by 'not recognising the body of the Lord', part at least of his meaning is that, through their factions and squabbles, their party spirit and polemics, they are refusing to recognise that the Church is Christ's one body.[18]

The Council of Trent had tragic reason to preface its Decree Concerning the Most Holy Sacrament of the Eucharist by saying that, having been convened in order to apply

> a remedy for all the heresies and the other most grievous troubles by which the Church of God is now miserably disturbed and rent into many and various parts, it would begin by eliminating errors regarding the Eucharist, which our Saviour left in his Church as a symbol of that unity and charity with which he wished all Christians to be mutually bound and united.[19]

---

18 See Tilliard, op. cit., pp. 113–16.
19 Denzinger-Bannwart-Rahner, 873 a.

Our own period in the history of the Church is one in which eucharistic prayer urgently needs once again to reflect deep-felt concern for unity and charity among Catholics. We must, whether at Mass or in eucharistic adoration, listen, all of us together, to the words of the Lord which clearly include a reference to the Eucharist: 'Father, may they be one in us as you are in me and I am in you, so that the world may believe it was you who sent me' (Jn 17:21). A concomitant of this concern and prayer for unity between Catholics around the Eucharist will be a prayerful longing for the wider unity between all Christians. There are moving pages about eucharistic worship and unity in the encyclical *Mystici Corporis*.

PASTORAL ORIENTATIONS

If the theological criteria for authentic eucharistic devotion which I have considered in this and the previous chapter are to be better applied in practice, certain pastoral directions should recommend themselves. We have seen, following Vonier, that eucharistic adoration is a prolongation of Mass and is destined to culminate in Holy Communion. It is perfectly true, as Rahner remarks, that Christ is present in the Blessed Eucharist as food to be eaten, and adoration of his adorable presence should keep this in view:

> The more clearly the reverent adoration of Christ in the sacrament is referred back to the eating of the body of Christ, the more eucharistic piety corresponds to the full truth and reality of the sacrament.[20]

We should, however, remember that, as we find so clearly in St John's Gospel, the 'eating of the body of Christ' includes faith and contemplation as well as sacramental Communion.

---

20   *Theological Investigations*, IV, p. 293.

Pastorally, therefore, exposition should, as far as possible, ensue from Mass – the exposed host being consecrated at that Mass. In monasteries and convents of perpetual adoration, exposition must, of course, now be interrupted during the celebration of Mass, at least in the sense that Mass may not be offered in the presence of the Blessed Sacrament exposed. This gives an opportunity for consecrating each day anew the sacred host for veneration during the next twenty-four hours. This provides a not unimportant reminder that adoration of the host is prolongation of the daily sacrifice and Communion.

Some responsible people advise that the monstrance for exposition should be left on the altar itself, so as to establish, even visually, the continuity between sacrifice and adoration. I have no desire to put my head in the hornet's nest of the discussion regarding the proper placing of the tabernacle, but I have been struck by the fact – and I pass it on for discussion – that two such different theologians as Karl Rahner and Eric Mascall questioned the desirability of systematically separating altar and tabernacle. Rahner says:

> The sacrament which remains after the sacrifice points much more impressively and, because of the divine institution, much more objectively to the past sacrifice and the future sacrificial meal than does the altar alone. And when the two signs are combined, the altar and the sacrificial food resting upon it, then this gives us, in the most impressive possible way, a sign in space and time, of divine institution, that Christ has sacrificed himself and now approaches us as our salvation uniting itself to us.[21]

Mascall wrote:

> [The method of reservation] whereby the consecrated elements are placed in a safe in the Church wall and removed from

---

21   On Developing Eucharistic Devotion, a text of 1959, in *Mission and Grace*, I, pp. 317–18.

association with the altar seems calculated to encourage almost every wrong view of the reserved sacrament that is conceivable.[22]

Benediction is now to be regarded as a short period of exposition, and the conducting of it should allow for and provide for appropriate prayers before the Blessed Sacrament. St Thomas' hymns and prayers, traditionally integral to Benediction, are excellent. But for all forms of eucharistic adoration – Benediction, Exposition, Holy Hours, Forty Hours' Prayer, Visits – we should exploit the liturgical offices of the Blessed Eucharist, especially their psalms, antiphons and Bible readings. We should call upon the liturgy of the Eucharist generally, we should explore the rich veins of Old Testament associations in St John's eucharistic and paschal chapters and in the Synoptic and Pauline teaching on the Eucharist and the Christian Pasch. We should also cultivate a strong ecclesial sense among our people. Pope Paul VI put it thus in *Mysterium Fidei*:

> The eucharistic sacrament, Venerable Brothers, is the sign and the cause of the unity of the mystical body, and it inspires an active 'ecclesial' spirit in those who venerate it with greater fervour. Therefore never cease to persuade those committed to your care that they should learn to make their own the cause of the Church, in approaching the eucharistic mystery; to pray to God without interruption; to offer themselves to God as a pleasing sacrifice for the peace and unity of the Church, so that all the children of the Church be united and think the same, that there be no divisions among them, but rather unity of mind and purpose, as the apostles insist (cf. 1 Cor 1:10).[23]

The proper liturgical model for eucharistic processions is surely the liturgy of Holy Thursday. The procession issues from the Mass, leads

---

22   *Corpus Christi*, p. 264.
23   *Mysterium Fidei*, n. 70.

to adoration and culminates in Holy Communion. There would seem to be good reasons for arranging that, if possible, any eucharistic procession should similarly be preceded directly by Mass, in which the host to be venerated will be consecrated. There have been suggestions, which do not seem at all romantic, that, in the course of the procession, Holy Communion might be carried to the sick in their homes, or, if they are not housebound, at 'altars of repose' along the route, where the sick could also be blessed with the Sacred Host.

The eucharistic procession is a particularly dramatic recall of the biblical truth of the abiding presence of God among his pilgrim people on the march through life and through history. It is a vivid demonstration of our will to 'eucharistify' and Christify our daily lives and work, our places of business, work and pleasure, our cities or our fields. They are, writes Rahner, our way of traversing with a view to sacralising 'the terrestrial dimensions of our existence'. He goes on:

> Processing through the places which form the context of their daily life … Christians wish to carry with them – and even to show – that which is the hidden spring of all the coming and going of their existence amid the world of change and flux. The procession is the symbol of that life of movement, yet also its answer: for the procession holds the fixed term of all movement, in a reality which does not change. Christians wish thus to show what is already the sign and promise, indeed the sacramental presence, of that for which all the labour and movement of life is waiting: eternal redemption, infinite rest, indestructible life … it is as though Christians, processing thus around the blocks and buildings of their towns and cities, wished to bring together, face to face, the everyday reality of their urban life, with all its nerve-wracking worldliness, and the holy reality mysteriously hidden in the tabernacles of our churches …[24]

---

24 'O Sacrum Convivium', *L'Eucharistie et les hommes d'aujourdhui*, pp. 29–30.

I shall end with words from *Lumen Gentium*:

> The priest alone can complete the building up of the body in the eucharistic sacrifice. Thus are fulfilled the words of God, spoken through his prophet: 'From the rising of the sun to the going down my name is great among the Gentiles, and in every place there is sacrifice, and there is offered to my name a clean oblation' (Mal 1:11). In this way the Church simultaneously prays and labours in order that the entire world may become the people of God, the body of the Lord, and the temple of the Holy Spirit, and that in Christ, the head of all, there may be rendered to the creator of the universe all honour and glory.[25]

---

25 *Lumen Gentium*, n. 17.

CHAPTER 5

THE EUCHARIST AND THE LAST THINGS

'The Four Last Things' were traditionally enumerated as 'death, judgement, hell, heaven'. These realities were associated in the minds of older generations with sermons regularly included in the mission and retreat programmes of parish and college and, for priests, seminary days and sermons which usually evoked anxiety and fear rather than hope and anticipation. Yet these great truths should really be seen by Christians as reasons for hope, and indeed for joyful hope. For beyond death and judgement lies the glorious Kingdom of our Risen Lord, Jesus Christ. At the end of the Nicene Creed, which we proclaim at Mass, we declare that we 'look for the resurrection of the dead and the life of the world to come'. The Latin word, *expectantes*, which we translate as 'we look for', carries the note of 'looking out for', almost of 'looking forward to'.[1] In each Mass we ask God in his Mercy to

> keep us free from sin
> and protect us from all anxiety,
> as we wait in joyful hope
> for the coming of Our Saviour, Jesus Christ.[2]

> For the Kingdom, the power and the glory are [his]
> now and for ever.

---

1 The creed in the third edition of the *Missal* translates *expectantes* as 'to look forward to' and thus reads: 'and I look forward to the resurrection of the dead'.
2 In the new *Missal* the wording has been changed to read: 'be always free from sin/and safe from all distress,/as we await the blessed hope/and the coming of our Saviour, Jesus Christ'.

DEATH

Yet the thought of death undoubtedly causes fear in all our hearts. Although, from the biological point of view, death is the inevitable end of all living bodies, something within us refuses to accept death as a natural event. The process of dying is biologically inseparable from the process of living – in a sense, we begin to die at birth – and yet we look on it as an unwelcome intrusion, something which 'ought not to happen'. Despite the many hundred deaths of which all of us have some personal knowledge, our own death or the death of those dear to us continues to cause sadness and even shock. It is true that we make a distinction between the death of an old person and the end of a young life; yet, even an old person's death is seen as something to be regretted and lamented.

In spite of the ubiquitousness of death, brought home to us every day in the 'death notices' page of our daily newspapers, we continue to resist the idea of death, sometimes even to protest against it. Some, like the poet Dylan Thomas, cry out: 'Do not go gentle into that good night,/Rage, rage, against the dying of the light.' Such rage would seem displaced and even futile; nevertheless the attitude which it expresses can be seen as a reflection of the scriptural teaching that death was not part of God's original plan for the human race, but was brought into the world by sin – the sin of our first parents. This was transmitted to all members of the human species through the solidarity which binds together all the descendants of he whom St Paul calls 'The first Adam' (cf.1 Cor 15:45). The rejection of the thought of death is also a reflection of the yearning for immortality that is part of the human condition. Even in pre-Christian times, and indeed in pre-historic times, that yearning seems to have existed in all the cultures of which we have knowledge. The ancient burial customs which archaeology has uncovered speak of belief in some sort of existence of an afterlife, in which there may still be need for food and where there may still be appreciation of beautiful and precious objects, all of which were often placed in the grave with the corpse or left on the grave subsequently. The same sense of an afterlife is expressed, however vaguely, in the burial practices that we find in secularist societies, which are often a parody of Christian burial rites.

Virgil wrote the poignant words *tendebantque manus ripae ulterioris amore* ('They stretched out their hands in longing for the further shore') and *sunt lacrimae rerum et mentem mortalia tangunt* ('There are tears in things and mortal things touch the soul'). The meaning clearly is that things which pass away touch the soul because of their fleetingness – for the soul craves for something that will last. The thought is similar to that of Pádraig Pearse, who wrote: 'The beauty of this world hath made me sad,/This beauty that will pass.' Also in a similar vein, Robert Browning wrote: 'And thus I know this earth is not my sphere./For I cannot so narrow me, but that/I still exceed it.'

Yet these yearnings for and intimations of immortality seem to be contradicted by the ineluctable fact of death. Does our Christian faith, does the Eucharist, resolve this dilemma? Do they offer a new explanation of death? In fact, faith in Christ does not offer a new theory of death, much less eliminate the sadness of death or even take away our natural resistance to the thought of death. Instead, Christ transforms death, even though he himself dreaded his own death, as his agonised prayer in the garden showed. He transforms it firstly by accepting death with all its 'wrenching pain': his own death was a particularly brutal and humiliating one, described in a remarkably objective way by the Gospel writers. The Passion narratives end with the burial of Jesus. It looked as though this was the final end of the life story of Jesus, as death is the final end of the life stories of all of us.

St Luke gives us a glimpse of the mood of all the followers of Jesus after his burial. Two of them were on the way to a village called Emmaus, presumably to resume their former occupations, which they had abandoned in order to follow Jesus. They walk along despondently, 'their faces downcast'. The whole Jesus chapter for them is now over, they speak of it in the past tense: 'Our own hope had been that he would be the one to set Israel free.' But now that is all over. Their whole body language speaks of disillusionment and defeat. There were strange stories about an empty tomb, but they dismissed them as ridiculous fantasies.

But the stories were not fantasies. The tomb was empty. Jesus, whom they had seen dying and then dead and buried, was alive. His death, freely and lovingly accepted for our sake, transforms our death into a life which will never die. Death becomes the passing over from mortal life into life everlasting. If we die with Christ, we shall live with him forever. Years afterwards, the risen Lord Jesus appears to John, the beloved disciple, on the island of Patmos, and says to him:

> Do not be afraid, it is I, the first and the last. I am the living One. I was dead and now I am alive and I am to live forever and ever; I hold the keys of death and of the underworld. (Rev 1:17)

That is the message of Jesus to us today. It is the message of the Risen and Ascended and Living Lord Jesus, really present in the Eucharist, to each of us who receive him, are touched by him in Holy Communion and who adore him on the altar at Mass, in the tabernacle or in the monstrance. When some of his followers grumbled about the Lord's 'intolerable language', about 'eating his flesh', he replied: '[But] what if you should see the Son of Man ascend to where he was before.' In other words, it is his resurrection and ascension that make it possible for his flesh to be real food and his blood real drink. His resurrected and ascended body is now free from the limitations of space and time and matter and mortality. His body and blood in the Eucharist can therefore interpenetrate our body, can permeate our whole being, to the point where we can become more and more one with him. When we eat ordinary bread we assimilate it into our body and brain and brawn; it becomes part of us. When we eat the Bread of Heaven, which is Christ, he assimilates our being into his; we become part of him. St Paul could say, 'The life I live now is not my own life, it is the life of Christ, living in me.' So, through Christ, the eucharistic life which we share becomes life everlasting. Our resurrection, brought about in us, is already beginning to happen. The life of the world to come is already present in us through our Holy Communion.

Two lives are going on side by side in the person reborn in Christ. There is the life of Christ in us, and there is our mortal life. When our mortal life ends, our other life continues in Christ, who lives in us and we in him forever and ever. We should not think of our soul as the part of us that lives in Christ and the body as not being in Christ. Our body too has been born into Christ in Baptism; it is anointed with Christ by the Holy Spirit in confirmation; it is touched and nourished by the Risen Christ in the Eucharist. Our body too is sanctified in Christ, consecrated by Christ and called by him to life everlasting through a share in his resurrection. St Paul says that whoever is in Christ is already a new creation, sharing even now in our mortal existence, in the new heavens and the new earth that will be fully revealed when Christ comes again in glory. St Paul says: 'When Christ is revealed, and he is your life, then you too will be revealed in all your glory with him.'

Death for the followers of Christ remains a hard fact. But for those who are 'in Christ' it is not the end of their life story, it is the beginning of real life, life without end. For believers in Christ, death does not have the last word; it has lost its victory and its sting. Through Christ's death on the cross – when he, the Living One, went to join humanity's myriad dead in the tomb – death is transformed into the anteroom of life everlasting. Pope John Paul once said that of all the billions of tombs that cover the surface of the earth, only one has seen the wonder of resurrection. The death of Mary, Mother of Jesus, has traditionally been seen as her 'dormition', the sleep from which she awakes into glory.

THE NEW CREATION

Above all is the certainty of Our Lord's victory, the sureness of the presence amongst us of his Glorified Body, the firm expectation of the new heaven and the new earth, already begun in him, already begun in us through our Baptism into his death and resurrection – this is what defines the manner of presence of the Church in the world and the manner of action of the Christian in the world. Everything we do must spring from this faith and reveal this hope. St Paul uses the word for citizenship (like our word for politics) when he urges the Philippians:

> You must exercise a citizenship worthy of Christ's Gospel; whether I come to see you, or only hear about you at a distance, this must be my news of you, that you are standing fast in a common unity of spirit, with the faith of the Gospel for your common cause. (Phil 1:27)

It is the resurrection that gives us the heart to work. It is at the end of the great chapter on the resurrection in First Corinthians that St Paul says:

> Stand firm, then, my beloved brethren, immovable in your resolve, doing your full share continually in the task the Lord has given you, since you know that in the Lord your labour is not in vain. (1 Cor 15:58)

This resurrection, in which we participate by our Baptism, is made 'really, truly and substantially' present for us in our Eucharist. Someone has said that on Sunday we Christians come to Mass 'to have the resurrection all over again'. In the Mass the new creation is already a reality. In the Eucharist, the transformation of the cosmos through the resurrection and ascension of Christ has already begun. The 'new heavens and the new earth' of the Book of Revelation are already here in the transubstantiated bread and wine of the Eucharist, now changed utterly into the Body and Blood of the Risen and Ascended Lord. The Eucharist is the first cell of the new creation. From our Lord's Risen Body, really present in the Eucharist, the new creation will one day burst forth upon the entire world.

Let me quote St Thomas Aquinas on the new heavens and the new earth, from the last chapter of the *Summa Contra Gentiles*:

When, therefore, the last judgement is completed, human nature will be entirely established in its goal. However, since everything bodily is somehow for the sake of man, at that time, also, the entire bodily creation will be changed – and suitably – to be in harmony with the state of the men who then will be. And because men will then be incorruptible, the state of generation and corruption will then be taken away from the whole bodily creation. And this is what the apostle says: that, 'the creature also itself shall be delivered from the servitude of corruption, into the liberty of the glory of the children of God' (Rom 8:21). Hence, one holds in accord with the faith that at the last the world will be purified by fire, not from corruptible bodies alone, but from that infection which the place incurred by serving as the dwelling of sinners. Since, then, the bodily creation will at the last be disposed in harmony with the state of man – since men, of course, will not only be freed from corruption but also clothed in glory, as what has been said makes clear – necessarily even the bodily creation will achieve a kind of resplendence in its own way.

And, hence, the saying of Revelations 21:1: 'I saw a new heaven and a new earth.' And Isaiah 65:17-18:

Behold I create new heavens, and a new earth: and the former things shall not be in remembrance and they shall not come upon the heart. But you shall be glad and rejoice forever.

If we have such a hope, if we really *believe* it, can any Marxist or humanist outdo us in human energy, enthusiasm, or dedication? Nietzsche's promethean man was to be an 'arrow of longing for the farther shore'. How much more is that true of the Christian? St Paul says:

> Not that I have already won the prize, already reached fulfilment. I only press on, in hope of winning the mastery, as Christ Jesus has won the mastery over me. No, brethren, I do not claim to have the mastery already, but this at least I do: forgetting what I have left behind, intent on what lies before me, I press on with the goal in view, eager for the prize, God's heavenly summons in Christ Jesus. (Phil 3:12-14)

MARY AND THE EUCHARIST

Mary has, since the early centuries of the Church, been associated with the Eucharist. The inscription carved on the tombstone of Abercius, Bishop of Hierapolis in Phrygia in the time of the Roman Emperor, Marcus Aurelius (161–180), is now preserved in the Lateran Museum. The inscription reads:

> I am Abercius, disciple of the Immaculate Shepherd. He taught me the doctrine of life and sent me to Rome ... Everywhere I found brethren united together ... Faith was always my guide and gave me as food the great fish, which the chaste virgin took from the spring; and possessing most excellent wine mixed with water along with bread.

At this time, of course, for fear of pagan mockery or sacrilege, Christians had to speak of the Eucharist in symbolic and veiled terms. The symbol of the fish is often used in the catacombs to represent Christ; sometimes the fish is shown as carrying on its back a basket of bread, occasionally with a flask of wine, as a symbol of the Eucharist. The Greek word for fish, *ichthus*, was often used as a synonym for Christ, its letters being the initials of the Greek words, 'Jesus Christ, Son of God, Saviour'.

A eucharistic miracle was reported to have occurred in Constantinople in the year 574, in the time of the Emperor Justinian. According to the story, a non-Christian child innocently consumed some consecrated bread. When he told his father what he had done, the father, who was a glass-blower, was enraged and threw the boy into the shop's blazing furnace. The mother, in desperation, dashed into the street to raise the alarm. People rushed in, but found the boy unscathed in the midst of the flames. They rescued him from the furnace and asked how he had survived the flames. He replied:

The woman who has a child in her arms and who is sitting down in the Church where I ate the bread of Christians, covered me with her cloak and kept the flames away from me.

The story – it may be only a legend – spread rapidly and is related by several writers, including Nicephorus in the East and St Gregory of Tours in the West. It at least reflects the connection that, from early centuries, the Church has seen between Mary and the Eucharist. I end with words spoken by Pope John Paul II when he was Cardinal Archbishop of Krakow. He was asked by Paul VI to preach the annual retreat to the Pope, cardinals and members of the Roman Curia. The retreat conferences he preached were published in a French translation with the title *Le signe de contradiction*, 'The Sign of Contradiction'. The whole volume expresses the soul of Pope John Paul II and the great themes of the papal ministry that, unknown to him, would be entrusted to him two years later. He ended his last retreat lecture with the words:

We have entered the last quarter of the two millennia which form the Christian era. It is like a new season of Advent for the Church, and for humanity. It is a time of waiting. But it is also a time of the Great Testing which has continued since that described in the third chapter of Genesis; only this time it is still more radical. It is the time of the Great Tribulation. It is also the time of the great Hope. To help us to live through this time we have been given a Sign, a sign of contradiction. The Sign is Mary, the Woman clothed with the Sun, the great sign which appeared in heaven, clothed with the sun, with the moon under her feet.

CHAPTER 6

IN A CRUMB OF BREAD THE MYSTERY

ST JOSEPH AND THE BLESSED SACRAMENT FATHERS

St Joseph is remarkable in that, although he played a central role in the mystery of the Incarnation, not one single word of his is recorded. In Jewish culture, Joseph was the one on whom the identity of Jesus as Messiah and as Son of David depended. The Messiah foretold by the prophets was to be Son of David, and it is through Joseph that Jesus is Son of David, for St Joseph, as both St Matthew's and St Luke's Gospels tell us, was 'of the House of David'. The words 'Joseph named him Jesus' are very important, for in Jewish law this meant that Jesus was legally the son of Joseph and therefore, through him, descended from King David. This was in spite of the fact that Joseph had no part in the conception of Jesus: because he was the husband of Mary, the Mother of Jesus, Joseph is truly the father of Jesus. We may note in passing that there was no expectation in Jewish tradition that the Messiah would be born of a virgin. On the contrary, he was expected to be born of the line of David in the ordinary way. The virginal birth of Jesus is not a story invented to fulfil an expectation, it is an historical fact, which at first sign conflicted with the general expectation. It was Joseph's acceptance of Jesus as his son that ensured that Jesus was son of Joseph – and therefore son of David and therefore Messiah.

This acceptance by Joseph was in obedience to God's wish as revealed to him in the dream recalled in the first chapter of Matthew's Gospel. When Joseph woke from the dream he said nothing, he just 'did what the angel of the Lord had told him to do' (Mt 1:24). In the same way, after the visit of the Wise Men and Herod's violent reaction, the angel of the Lord told Joseph in a dream to 'get up, take the child and his mother and escape into Egypt', so 'Joseph got up and took the child and his mother with him and left that very night for Egypt' (Mt 2:13). The same instant and unquestioning obedience of Joseph to God's will is repeated again after Herod's death. In almost identical words, Matthew tells us that the angel of the Lord appeared again in a dream and said to Joseph: 'Get up, take the child and his mother with you, and go back to the land of Israel' (Mt 2:20-1). Again, Joseph gets up and does exactly that: no questions are asked, no speeches made. Joseph does what God asks and that is all, but that is how Joseph plays his part in fulfilling God's eternal plan of salvation for the whole world. There is a lesson there for each one of us. A Church writer, speaking about the early Christians, said 'We don't *talk* big: we *act*.'

Pope John Paul issued an apostolic exhortation, *Redemptoris Custos*, on St Joseph early in his pontificate. This was in 1989, exactly one hundred years after Leo XIII, the great Pope of the workers, published an encyclical on St Joseph, called *Quamquam Pluries*. Pope John Paul called attention to St Joseph's faith and his silence. He remarked on how Joseph silently and contemplatively pondered on the mystery of Jesus, sharing in Mary's faith and wondering contemplation. Joseph thereby became guardian of the mystery of Jesus, the mystery hidden in the seemingly ordinary life of the Holy Family and in the ordinary work of the carpenter's shop at Nazareth. The Pope remarked that 'the silence [of Joseph] reveals in a special way the inner portrait of the man'. The Gospels, he continued, 'allow us to discover in his "actions" – shrouded in silence as they are – an aura of deep contemplation'.[1] This was why the great contemplative, St Teresa of Jesus, reformer of the Carmelite Order, felt it so important to renew devotion to St Joseph in the Church of her time.

A familiar prayer to St Joseph, which used to be recited after the rosary during the month of October, recalled 'the fatherly affection

---

1   John Paul II, *Redemptoris Custos*, Apostolic Exhortation on the Person and Mission of St Joseph on the Life of Christ and the Church (15 August 1989), n. 25.

with which [he] used to embrace the infant Jesus', and called Joseph 'provident guardian of the Holy Family'. All can be confident that now, in the glory of heaven, he will help us in our prayerful closeness to Jesus in the Eucharist, will watch over the whole family of the Church and defend it from all adversity.

THE REAL PRESENCE

Part of the adversity that faces the Church at the present time is widespread confusion about its teaching on many matters, and indeed considerable ignorance and misinformation about matters of faith. The doctrine of the real presence of the Body and Blood of the Lord Jesus Christ in the Eucharist – and consequently of the real change of the bread and wine into the Body and Blood of Jesus Christ, transubstantiation – is an essential and unchangeable dogma of Catholic faith. The Church cannot give up the doctrine because it is founded on the words of Jesus Christ himself, which have been taken seriously from the time of the early Church in both the East and West. Let the fourth-century St Cyril of Jerusalem speak for the East:

> Under the appearance of bread the Body is given to us and the Blood under the appearance of wine ... Do not regard this as mere bread and wine; they are the Body and Blood of Christ. Although the senses may tell you they are [bread and wine], faith assures you quite differently. Do not judge by the taste.[2]

Let St Ambrose, also of the fourth century, speak for the West:

> It is really the Body and Blood, because through the divine omnipotence, the bread and the wine are changed into the Body and Blood of Christ ... If the work of Elias made fire come down from heaven, will not the words of Christ be

---

2   St Cyril of Jerusalem, *Mystagogical Catechism*, 4.

able to effect a change of elements … [God] can bring forth from nothing what did not exist. Is he not then able to change existing things into what they were not before?[3]

This was the belief of the Church from the very beginning. At the end of the first century and at the beginning of the second, when people were still alive who had known the apostles, Tertullian, a brilliant intellectual Christian convert in the Church in north Africa, wrote about the practice of Christians in bringing home the consecrated host for Holy Communion outside of Mass. Speaking of the difficulties of Christian–pagan marriages in *Ad Uxorem*, he asks the Christian spouse: 'What will [your pagan husband think] you are eating secretly before you take any other food? And if he knows it is bread, will he not think it is just ordinary bread?'

Elsewhere, writing about the Eucharist, Tertullian says: 'We [Christians] are anxiously careful lest any drop from the Chalice or any particle from the bread should fall to the ground' (*De Corona*).

One of the great difficulties faced by Christians in those early times of the Church, living as they did in an overwhelmingly pagan society, was that they were the object of suspicion and malicious rumours of all kinds. Sometimes the rumours are revealing. One of the most persistent grew around the fact that Christians gathered in the evening by candlelight for the celebration of the Eucharist. Pagans overheard scraps of conversations among Christians, telling of how they called one another brother and sister and how together they received the Body and Blood of Jesus Christ. The pagan rumour factory turned this into a horror story, according to which Christians gathered for incestuous sexual orgies and feasted on the human flesh and blood of babies baked in flour. Christians were therefore accused of both incest and cannibalism. This was, of course, a gross calumny. Indirectly, however, it testifies to the fact that Christians believed that what they were receiving looked

---

3   St Ambrose, *De Mysteriis*, 50.

like bread or baked flour but, in reality, was the Body and Blood of Christ. This calumny could not have originated if the Christians believed that the consecrated bread was simply a symbol or a figure or a reminder of the Body of Christ. The realism of the Eucharistic faith of the earliest Christians is thus unwittingly attested by their pagan contemporaries.

We are living again in an age in which some find it difficult to accept the realism of Catholic faith in the Eucharist and in which even some Catholics seem, perhaps unknowingly, to blur and obscure the doctrine of the real presence of Christ in the Eucharist. But rejection of this doctrine goes back to the time of Christ himself. In the sixth chapter of St John's Gospel, we read that after Christ had affirmed his real and bodily presence in the bread and wine of the Eucharist, 'many of his followers said, "This is intolerable language. How could anyone accept it?"' Jesus knew of their complaints, and he said to them:

Does this upset you? What if you should see the Son of Man ascend to where he was before? It is the Spirit that gives life; the flesh has nothing to offer. The words I have spoken to you are spirit and they are life. (Jn 6:59-43)

Jesus is not withdrawing anything of what he had said when he stressed the realism of his bodily presence. He is simply giving the key to understanding how this is possible: it is possible because of his resurrection and ascension into heaven. Rising from the dead in the power of the Holy Spirit, the body of Jesus becomes, as St Paul puts it, 'life-giving Spirit' (cf. Cor 15:45). Through the resurrection and ascension, the body of Christ is raised above the limiting conditions of earthly life, which confined his body to one place at one time. Risen and ascended, he can be simultaneously in all places and at all times. This is what makes it possible for Christ to be really and bodily present, in his Spirit-filled body, on all the altars of the earth and in all the centuries of time. The resurrection enables Jesus Christ to be as close to each one present at Mass or adoring before the Eucharist as he was close to the apostles who walked with him, talked with him and ate with him in Galilee and Jerusalem, or felt his supporting arm around them in the boat on the Sea of Galilee.

This passage in St John's Gospel is strikingly similar to his account of Jesus' appearing, after the resurrection, to Mary Magdalene in the garden near the tomb where his body had been laid. At first she does not recognise him, thinking he is the gardener. But, when Jesus addressed her personally as 'Mary', she knew him immediately. Rushing to him, she tightly clasped his feet, determined that never again would anyone be able to take the body of the Lord away from her. But Jesus says to her:

> Do not cling to me, because I have not yet ascended to my Father. But go and find the brothers, and tell them: I am ascended to my Father, and to your Father, to my God and to your God. (Jn 20:11-18)

Once again, Jesus is telling us that his resurrection and his ascension will make it possible for him to be as close to every single brother- and sister-disciple, in every place and through all time, as he then was to Mary Magdalene when she clung tightly to his body. He is telling her that there is no need to cling to him with her hands because, once he has ascended to the Father, she will cling to him still more closely by faith – for the clasp of faith is tighter and more close and more strong and unbreakable than the clasp of bodily hands.

It is the resurrection, therefore, that makes Christ's presence in the Eucharist possible; and it is the Eucharist that makes the resurrection present. The resurrection is made present to the clasp of each one of us, wherever we gather to celebrate the Eucharist in memory of him. When we come to celebrate the Eucharist, and when we pray before the Holy Sacrament, we are having the Resurrection as well as the

Passion all over again. A familiar 'soul hymn' asks: 'Were you there when they crucified my Lord? ... Were you there when he rose up from the tomb?' When we are present at Mass and at adoration, we can truly say, 'Yes I was', 'Yes I am.' When, with the Church, we 'do this in memory' of Jesus, the Passion is made sacramentally present, the Resurrection is sacramentally re-enacted in our presence. The Crucified and Risen and Ascended Lord is really and truly present in all the power and efficacy of the Paschal Mystery, whereby he passed from this world to the Father (cf. Jn 13:1) in order that we, with him, might one day pass from this world to the place he has prepared for us in the Father's house (cf. Jn 14:2-3).

IN A CRUMB OF BREAD

The resurrection, St Paul tells us, is the very foundation of our faith. It is also the foundation of the Eucharist, the 'mystery of faith'. The resurrection and ascension make it possible for the whole mystery of our faith to be concentrated in 'a crumb of bread'. In 'The Great Hunger', Patrick Kavanagh wrote lines which reflect part of the culture which surrounds us today, even more than it did in the poet's own: 'As Respectability ... knows the price of all things/And marks God's truth in pounds and pence and farthings.' But he then turns to watch farming people hurrying to Mass:

> Five hundred hearts were hungry for life –
> Who lives in Christ shall never die the death.
> And the candle-lit Altar and the flowers
> And the pregnant Tabernacle lifted a moment to Prophecy
> Out of the clayey hours ...

Later in the poem he speaks of people who are 'picking up life's truth singly' while Maguire, the man whose 'mystical imagination' is the subject of the poem (and is perhaps to be identified with its author), speaks of

> ... the Absolute envased bouquet –
> All or nothing. And it was nothing. For God is not all
> in one place, complete and labelled like a case in a railway store
> Till Hope comes in and takes it on his shoulder –
> O Christ, that is what you have done for us:
> In a crumb of bread the whole mystery is.[4]

'In a crumb of bread the whole mystery is', for the bread is no longer bread but it is changed into the Body of Christ. The Catholic Church teaches, as a matter of divinely revealed faith, that the whole substance of bread is changed into the substance of the Body of Christ, and the whole substance of wine into the substance of Christ's Blood. The Council of Trent added that this change is 'appropriately and properly called transubstantiation'. It is not the word which is the dogma, but the real change of substance.

It is said that the word and the theory of transubstantiation were introduced only in medieval times. But this is not the point; the point is the real change of the identity of the bread and wine into the identity of the Body and Blood of Christ. That is what the dogma means and this has been the faith of the Church from the time of the apostles. It is shared by the Eastern Churches, which so pride themselves on fidelity to the faith handed on by the apostles; it is based on the actual words of Christ himself. The term 'transubstantiation' had many equivalents in the early centuries. I have quoted St Ambrose, who speaks of 'a change of elements'. Other terms, such as 'transelementation', 'transformation', 'refashioning', 'conversion' and 'transmutation', were used by the Church, both in the East and West, from the earliest centuries. The truth contained in the term 'transubstantiation' is most certainly an integral part of 'the Catholic faith that comes to us from the apostles'.

---

4   Patrick Kavanagh, 'The Great Hunger', *Collected Poems* (London: Allen Lane; 2004), p. 69, p. 72.

It is said that the doctrine of transubstantiation is an attempt to *explain* the mystery of the presence of Christ in the Eucharist. This is not so: the doctrine is not a statement of the *how* of the Real Presence; instead it is a clear and unqualified affirmation of the *that* of the true, real and substantial presence of the Body and Blood of Jesus Christ in the Holy Eucharist. I want to quote from another Irish writer, Kate O'Brien. In her novel, *The Ante-Room*, she describes the feelings of a priest at the moment of consecration of a Mass offered in a sick room (the novel is set in the days of the Latin Mass):

> There was only in him as he spoke his Latin an entirely cold and calm understanding that God was in his hands … He only said the words the Church ordained to him and was aware, without cloud or pang or question, of the everlasting miracle, *Mysterium Fidei* [The Mystery of Faith]. Silence relaxed into quietude. God was present; the room and the morning were full of peace.

EUCHARIST ADORATION

In the silence and peace of the presence of the Blessed Sacrament in the Tabernacle, each one who adores tries to turn that 'cold and calm understanding' into the warm and loving embrace of the Lord, who showed us what love means by dying for us on the Cross. Eating is a very powerful way of changing another substance into our own. Food, when eaten and digested, is transformed into our own flesh and bone and brain cells. But when we eat the bread which is the Body and Blood of Christ, it is Christ who transforms us into himself, making us into the Christ-persons which our name 'Christian' calls us to be, and indeed presupposes that we are. Baptism is sometimes called 'Christening'; this is a very meaningful word: *Christ*ening, it means our becoming transformed into Christ. The Eucharist is a most powerful means for being thus transformed into Christ. Julian of Norwich spoke of being 'substantially oned' with Christ. The purpose of adoration of the Most Blessed Sacrament is to become more and more 'substantially oned' with Christ, so that, as St Paul puts it, for us to live is Christ, and the life we live is the 'life of Christ who lives in us' (cf. Gal 2:20).

In our adoration, we are already living the same life which we are to live forever in God's presence in heaven – a life of love and praise of 'God's glory shining in the face of Christ' (2 Cor 4:6), a life of wonder and admiration and astonishment and indeed surprise at the Truth of Beauty and Splendour of Truth and the overpowering but deliciously transforming and healing 'Weight of Glory' (cf. 2 Cor 4:17) that awaits us when this life's adoration is changed into the eternal adoration of heaven. Paul Durcan has a marvellous phrase: 'Heaven … is a place …/That would surprise you.'[5] Heaven is endlessly repeated surprise at the unveiled beauty hidden in the mysteries we now know – faintly and darkly but truly – by faith. This has rarely been better expressed than in the concluding verse of St Thomas Aquinas's great hymn, *Adoro Te*:

> Jesus, whom in this life I see hidden by a veil,
> I pray that what I so ardently long for may come to pass,
> that one day I may see your face unveiled
> and be filled for ever with delight at the full revelation
> of your glory.

Another Irish writer, Frank O'Connor, describing what he felt at the death of his mother, who had prayed fervently all her life, had not words more appropriate than the words of Psalm 16:

> As for me, in my justice I shall see your face,
> and be filled when I awake
> with the sight of your glory. [6]

---

5   Paul Durcan, 'Brazilian Presbyterian', *Greetings to Our Friends in Brazil* (London: Harvill Press, 1999).

6   Frank O'Connor, from *An Only Child, An Only Child and My Father's Son: An Autobiography* (London: Penguin, 2005).